EVERYDAY

WICCA

Also by Gerina Dunwich

Candlelight Spells
The Concise Lexicon of the Occult
Circle of Shadows (poetry)
Wicca Craft
Wicca Love Spells (*The Secrets of Love Magick*)
The Wicca Spellbook
The Wicca Book of Days
The Wicca Garden
The Wicca Source Book
Wicca Candle Magick (*The Magick of Candle Burning*)
A Wiccan's Guide to Prophecy and Divination

EVERYDAY

WICCA

MAGICKAL SPELLS THROUGHOUT THE YEAR

GERINA DUNWICH

Citadel Press
Kensington Publishing Corp.
www.kensingtonbooks.com

CITADEL PRESS books are published by

Kensington Publishing Corp.
850 Third Avenue
New York, NY 10022

All Kensington titles, imprints, and distributed lines are available at special quantity discounts for bulk purchases for sales promotions, premiums, fund raising, educational, or institutional use. Special book excerpts or customized printings can also be created to fit specific needs. For details, write or phone the office of the Kensington special sales manager: Kensington Publishing Corp., 850 Third Avenue, New York, NY 10022, attn: Special Sales Department, phone 1-800-221-2647.

Kensington and the K logo Reg. U.S. Pat. & TM Office
Citadel Press is a trademark of Kensington Publishing Corp.

First printing 1997

10 9 8 7 6 5

Printed in the United States of America

ISBN 0-8065-1869-3

Cataloging data for this publication can be obtained from the Library of Congress.

I dedicate this book with love to my
mother, and especially to Al.
Thank you both for always
being there for me.

CAST A SPELL

Within a circle of white light
cast a spell—the time is right.
Invoke the powers, one by one
in harmony with Moon and Sun.
Light a candle; burn it bright,
cast a spell with all your might.
If the Rede you never shun,
then true your magick shall be done.

Gerina Dunwich

CONTENTS

INTRODUCTION

———•———

Have you ever wanted to cast a spell? Perhaps you already have without even being aware of it! For example, simple acts such as making a wish on a falling star or throwing a pinch of salt over your shoulder to avert bad luck are customs that have actually evolved from ancient Pagan religious beliefs and practices, and could be considered two basic acts of spellcasting.

Of course the mere making of a wish or the throwing of salt into the air does not in itself make one a Witch, but they are both examples of how simple folk magick works.

To make these mundane gestures into a true act of magick, all one would need to do is perform it with visualization and intent.

For instance, to add magick to the wish made on a star, you would need to visualize the wish coming true as it is being spoken in the form of a spell (or prayer to the Goddess and/or the Horned God) for the desired outcome. Example:

HARMING NONE AND RESPECTING THE FREE WILL OF ALL LIVING THINGS, IT IS MY WILL AND INTENT TO

(state whatever it is you are wishing to attain or accomplish.)
To seal the spell, the phrase:

SO MOTE IT BE

would then be said.

The five-pointed star known as a pentacle is a sacred symbol of the magickal craft of Wicca. (When written or drawn it is called a pentagram.) It represents wo/man (the spirit or the divine) and the four ancient elements of Air, Fire, Water, and Earth. It is used, among other things, for protection, invoking, controlling, and banishing elemental forces.

To add magick to the gesture of throwing salt over your shoulder, you would need to visualize yourself surrounded by a protective sphere of Goddess/God energy in the form of white light. Once this was done and as the salt was being cast into the air, you would recite a spell such as:

WITH THIS SALT, A SYMBOL OF THE SACRED EARTH AND A TOOL OF PURIFICATION, I DO HEREBY BANISH ALL ENERGIES NEAR AND FAR THAT ARE OF A NEGATIVE NATURE. I AM NOW, AND SHALL ALWAYS BE, PROTECTED BY THE SPHERE OF WHITE LIGHT. THIS IS MY WILL. SO MOTE IT BE.

The first and perhaps the most important thing to remember when casting a spell of any kind is the Wiccan Rede. This is the creed of contemporary Neo-Pagan Witchcraft which states: "Eight words the Wiccan Rede fulfill; An' it harm none, do what ye will."

What this means simply is do not use magick or any other type of energy or power to bring deliberate harm unto others, including yourself. Never attempt to manipulate or interfere with the free will of any living thing.

If you should violate the Wiccan Rede (even unintentionally or through carelessness) you will have to pay a price: The negativity created by your own actions will return to you threefold or more. This applies to all spells you cast, regardless of how simple they may seem. (More about this in a bit when I discuss what is known as Dark Magick.)

And speaking of simple spells: Just as magick can be as simple as one desires, it can also be as complicated as one chooses. But while an elaborate ritual employing lots of expensive and/or difficult to obtain magickal paraphernalia may indeed be quite a flashy show (and there is absolutely nothing wrong with this), it certainly is not requisite for performing effective magick.

A simple spell using just a candle can often be just as powerful if it is done with the right intent and if it is magick that is drawn from the most important source—straight from the heart.

I often receive interesting letters from people around the world (many of them young folks) who are interested in Wicca and are new to the art of spellcasting. Many want to know if there is any way that they (or I on their behalf) can cast a spell or concoct a magickal potion to instantly solve all of their problems, make them win the lottery, literally transform them into a different person, and other impossibilities. I've even been sent letters by incarcerated criminals inquiring if I, for a fee, would be willing to perform a spell of some sort to get them released from prison.

As with anything else, there are certain things that magick can do and certain things that it cannot. One must not jump blindly into magickal workings with unrealistic expectations and/or selfish motives. To do so is only setting yourself up for a disappointment.

As far as spellcasting is concerned, you must first acquire a basic understanding of magick and how it actually works. It is an extremely powerful energy that can bring about a desired change when used correctly (being performed during the appropriate lunar phase and using herbs possessing the correct magickal or astrological vibrations, for example.) But as much as we would all like to wave our magick wands, and then "poof!" . . . something we want just suddenly appears, we must face the fact that it unfortunately does not work that way in real life. The "Samantha Stevens" type of magick is not realistic.

This is not to say that the magick real-life Witches work with is not powerful, because it truly is. It just happens to work in a different way.

Magick can help you but it will not solve all of your personal problems if you are not willing to put some hard work and effort into the betterment of your own life. Magick can awaken your inner strength and keep you focused on your goals, but the rest is up to you. If a spell helps to create an opportunity for you but you do nothing to act upon it, chances are nothing good will come of it.

If you are one of those people who are plagued with constant problems or what appears to be a streak of bad luck, magick can help to banish negativity, attract good luck into your life, even break curses (if they are responsible), and protect you against psychic attacks.

However, if the same problems continue to arise after trying all manners of magick to combat them, perhaps it is time for you to examine (or reexamine) your situation to find out just why you seem to be a magnet for attracting them. Is it something you are possibly bringing on yourself without even being aware of it? Perhaps you simply need to make some positive adjustments in your life or learn to handle your situations in a better way so they do not reoccur.

Regarding the lottery, the simple reason that no amount of magick can win the lottery for you is because there are countless numbers of people just like yourself wishing, hoping, and praying (each a form of magick) for different numbers to come up. The end result is nothing more than a conflict of magickal energies. As each person who gambles on a lottery ticket focuses their energies on his or her personal numbers, these energies are simultaneously working against the energies of the next person, and so on, and so on. Magickally, it is a no-win situation as only one set of numbers at a time can be drawn as the winner.

I have no doubt in my mind that if everyone who purchased a lottery ticket played the same numbers, that combination would come up. But of course a million dollar jackpot being divided between several million players would not amount to very much. It wouldn't even make up for the cost of each person's lottery ticket.

Transformations are another aspect of magick which many people have lots of questions and misunderstandings about. I've often been asked if magick can be used to physically transform a person, such as changing their weight, height, eye color, and so forth.

Wanting to make personal changes to better one's appearance is fine. In fact I think it's only normal for most people to be dissatisfied with one or more things about their bodies. But again, one must be realistic in one's approach to, and expectations of, the magickal transformation of physical traits.

If, for instance, you wish to lose weight, a spell can help you stay on your diet, strengthen your willpower to resist overeating or indulging in the wrong foods, and so forth. But no spell or magick potion can make you miraculously shed twenty-five pounds within the blink of an eye! You must always work toward your goals. Magick is not an easy way out. It is simply a way of putting things into motion.

As far as changing one's height and eye color, platform shoes and colored contact lenses would probably be more suitable solutions.

We all must accept that there are certain things in this life that cannot and should not be changed. Being able to accept these things is the first step toward true spiritual harmony.

Transformative magick does not literally mean transforming your physical being like Doctor Jeckyll turning into Mister Hyde. The word "transformation" refers instead to your spiritual self. Growing spiritually means changing negative into positive, changing destructive into constructive, becoming a happier, healthier, more productive person, putting what is out of balance back into balance, and so forth.

"What's a good spell for this?" and "What's a good spell for that?" are also questions I'm asked frequently. There is certainly no shortage of spells, as a few minutes spent browsing through the Occult/New Age section of just about any large bookstore or library in this country will confirm. But what exactly is it that makes a "good spell" really a good spell? The answer is rather simple: In my opinion, any spell is a good spell if you feel comfortable performing it, if it brings no harm whatsoever to anyone, and if you believe in yourself and can focus and direct your power properly once it has been raised. This can take some practice and patience, so try not to become discouraged if you do not experience immediate results.

In this book you will learn how to use positive energy to work magick with effective results. You will be shown how to properly cast and uncast a magick circle, how to work in harmony with the different phases of the moon, how to use poetry for spellwork, divination, and healing; and much more.

I have also put together a section of spells and rituals (with both novice and seasoned Witches in mind) for use throughout the course of a year. The magick in this book is designed for solitaries (Witches who work magick alone either by choice or by

chance) and covens alike. It is Wiccan in nature and of a positive path only. Nowhere in this book will you find any Dark Magick.

DARK MAGICK

The term "dark magick" is used to describe both black magick (also known as the art of sorcery) and gray magick, which is basically any type of magick that is not of a white nature.

White magick, also referred to as "true magick," is the type of magick most Wiccans and contemporary Pagans choose to practice. It is magick that is positive, and used mainly for the good of others, for healing, love matters, spiritual growth, and beneficial transformations. White magick harms none and is consistent with the Wiccan Rede. The opposite of white magick is, of course, black magick (which is a term nearly everyone is familiar with). Even those who possess a limited understanding of the Craft are aware that black magick deals with such negative things as curses, hexes, sticking pins into dolls, the summoning of demonic energies, the manipulation of others against their own free will, and basically any spell cast with a deliberate evil intent.

Black magick is very powerful, and also extremely dangerous to even toy with. Unfortunately it is also very enticing, especially to those who seek revenge against others, power over others, or the attainment of selfish whims and desires.

It is this false promise of power without cost and the idea of greedy wishes granted that lures the naïve into the darkness like flies to a spider's web. Once trapped in it, the unsuspecting will find themselves rapidly heading down the road to self-destruction because whatever harmful energy one sends out to others is returned to the sender three times as strong.

This threefold karmic retribution is known as the Threefold Law, or Law of Three. It works every time you do something bad, even if you do not believe in magick or Karma. The Threefold Law also works every time you do something good. Whatever you do will come back to you three times, so doing good is more preferable than doing evil. So be sure to always think twice before you cast any spell, and make it a point to use magick only in a positive and constructive fashion.

Too often have I seen individuals playing sorcerer and foolishly conjuring up things that are better off left alone. These misguided souls always end up regretting it in one way or another.

When a very close friend of mine first began to practice the art of spellcraft, she (like many other young and naïve Witches who start out by reading the wrong books) tried her luck in dabbling a bit with negative energies. Not surprisingly, she discovered that something bad always seemed to happen to her afterward. It took awhile before she finally arrived at the realization that it was she herself who was creating her own misfortunes through her actions. By sending out darkness, she received darkness in return. However, when she began to work only with positive energies and light, the bad luck cycle immediately ceased.

The moral of this story is: It is easy to get lost in the darkness, but only in the light can you find your way. The choice is up to you.

Gray magick is a type of magick that incorporates the elements of both positive and negative. White magick that borders on being black (such as love spells that are designed to magickally manipulate the emotions of another against their will) are generally considered to be in the category of gray magick.

Although gray magick is not considered by most to be as wicked as black magick, it nevertheless contradicts the Wiccan Rede; therefore, karmic consequences of one sort or another must inevitably be faced by those who choose to work with it.

The inverted pentacle or pentagram is generally regarded as the symbol of black magick and Satanism; however, in certain Wiccan circles it is used to represent the Horned God (male principle of the Supreme Deity and consort of the Goddess) or to denote the second-degree rank.

EVERYDAY

WICCA

Chapter 1

LUNAR SPELLWORK

"Moon-Woman, old and wise.
Hair of silver; pale gray eyes.
She rises high above the night,
spinning spider silk of light,
shining like a beacon bright
to light the way for faeries' flight."

The moon, along with its phases, energies, and symbols, possesses a strong influence over all rites of magick in the Witchcraft of modern times, just as it has done so in the past.

It is connected to the monthly menstrual cycle of women (in certain cultures, the words used for "moon" and "menstrual" are identical or closely related) and continues to be viewed by many as a sacred symbol of the great Goddess, woman-magick, and female energy. The moon is also associated with the mysteries of the dark and the ocean tides, and repre-

sents intuition, the psychic powers of the mind, emotion, mood, fertility, and even lunacy.

To perform successful magick, it is important to always work in harmony with the moon and its different lunar phases. All types of spellwork must be performed during their corresponding lunar phase or else they will be ineffective.

In certain cases, if a specific spell is cast during the incorrect lunar phase, it can actually result in the magick doing just the opposite of what it was intended to do. For instance, if you were to cast a spell for increasing money during a waning moon instead of during a waxing moon—which would be the correct lunar phase for this type of spell—it is highly possible that the spell would backfire and cause you to actually lose money instead of gaining it!

WAXING MOON

A waxing moon (the time from the new moon, through the first quarter, to the full moon) corresponds to the Maiden (also

Warrior and Virgin) aspect of the Triple Goddess, and is the proper time for performing rituals in honor of Her.

It is also the appropriate lunar phase during which to perform spells and rituals involving all forms of growth, strengthening, and the increasing of things (such as love, good luck, health, money, and so forth.)

FULL MOON

The energy of the full moon increases a Witch's psychic powers; therefore, the full moon phase is said to be the most favorable time of all to perform divinations as well as spells and rituals that increase psychic abilities and induce dreams that reveal the future or the unknown.

The full moon corresponds with the Mother aspect of the Triple Goddess, making it also a powerful phase for working all manners of fertility magick.

The moon has been associated with female fertility since antiquity, and at one time it was commonly believed that if a woman desired children, she could simply sleep under the silvery-white light of the moon and become magickally impregnated by a moonbeam.

Full moons also enhance the power of spells that involve creativity, nurturing, and sensuality.

WANING MOON

A waning moon (the time from the full moon, through the last quarter, to the new moon) corresponds to the Crone aspect of the Triple Goddess, and is the proper lunar phase in which to perform spells and rituals that bring things to an end. This is the correct time to reverse spells (countermagick), and decrease, banish, and destroy things (such as diseases, addictions, a streak of bad luck, and so forth).

Witches performing a circle dance beneath the full moon. (Fortean Picture Library)

Crone-honoring rites are traditionally performed during the waning of the moon, as this is the time of the month that the powers of the Crone (also known as the Dark Goddess) are at their greatest. The Crone represents maturity of wisdom, spiritual peace, a time of endings that lead to new beginnings, and death that brings forth new life.

Nearly all spells of a positive nature are performed during the waxing of the moon, while most spells of a negative nature are performed during the waning of the moon and most spells of a psychic or divinatory nature are performed during the full of the moon. (The thirteen full moons that occur each year are also the traditional times for most covens' esbats, which are monthly meetings during which a Goddess and/or Horned God honoring rite is usually performed, along with magick workings, healings [as necessary], and the taking care of general coven business.)

The terms "positive" and "negative" are not necessarily used to indicate white (or good) and black (or bad) magick. Rather, positive means that which constructs, strengthens, or attracts; and negative means that which destroys, weakens, or banishes.

Also, like the opposite charges of a battery or the opposite poles of a magnet, there are positives and negatives throughout the four elements and the twelve astrological signs of the zodiac. The elements of Fire and Air are said to be positive, while Earth and Water are negative. The six signs of the zodiac classified as positive are: Aries, Gemini, Leo, Libra, Sagittarius, and Aquarius. The negative signs are the remaining six: Taurus, Cancer, Virgo, Scorpio, Capricorn, and Pisces.

Additionally, positive also corresponds to the yang/masculine/active energies, and negative corresponds to the yin/feminine/passive energies.

SPELLWORK BY LUNAR PHASE

The following is a list of different types of spellwork (arranged in alphabetical order), followed by the appropriate lunar phase/s during which each one should be performed. (If you are ever in doubt as to which phase of the moon is the correct one for a certain spell, I would recommend performing it on a night when the moon is full because this is the time when the power of magick is greatest.)

ABUNDANCE: waxing to full moon.
ADDICTIONS (TO END):   waning moon.
ARTISTIC CREATIONS: waxing to full moon.
BAD HABITS (to break):   waning moon.

BAD LUCK (to reverse): waning moon.
BEAUTY AND HEALTH: full moon.
BINDINGS: waning moon.
BLESSINGS: full moon.
CAREER ADVANCEMENT: waxing moon.
COMMUNICATION: full moon.
CURSES, HEXES (to break): waning moon.
DIVINATIONS: waxing and full moons.
ENERGY RAISING: waxing moon.
EXORCISMS: waning moon.
FEAR (overcoming): waning moon.
FERTILITY RITUALS: waxing and full moons.
FORGIVENESS: new moon.
FRIENDSHIP: waxing moon.
GARDEN PLANTING SPELLS: waxing moon.
GOALS (attainment of): waxing to full moon.
GOOD LUCK: waxing moon.
GROWTH (of any kind): waxing moon.
HARMONY: waxing moon.
HAPPINESS: waxing and full moons.
HEALINGS (to increase health): waxing moon.
HEALINGS (to end sickness): waning moon.
HOUSE BLESSINGS: full moon.
INSPIRATION: waxing and full moons.
INTUITION: full moon.
JINX-BREAKING: waning moon.
JUDGMENT: waxing and full moons.
LIBERATION (to free oneself from something): waning moon.
LOVE MAGICK: waxing and full moons.
LOVE SPELLS (to reverse): waning moon.
LUNAR GODDESS INVOCATIONS: full moon.
MONEY MATTERS (to increase wealth): waxing moon.
NEGATIVITY (to banish): waning moon.

NIGHTMARES (to banish):   waning moon.

OBTAINING (things and goals):   waxing and full moons.

OMENS: full moon.

OVERCOMING: waning moon.

PEACE (to end hostility, war):   waning moon.

POWER: waxing and full moons.

PROPHETIC DREAMS: full moon.

PROTECTION: waxing moon.

PSYCHIC POWERS (developing, strengthening):   full moon.

QUESTS: new moon.

REAL ESTATE (to buy):   waxing moon.

REAL ESTATE (to sell):   waning moon.

SEXUAL DESIRES (to stimulate, increase):   waxing moon.

SHAPESHIFTING: full moon.

SPIRIT CONJURATIONS: full moon.

STRENGTH: waxing moon.

TEACHING: waxing and full moons.

TRANSFORMATIONS: full moon.

TRAVEL: waxing moon.

UNIONS (marriages, business partnerships):   waxing and full moons.

WEATHERWORKINGS (to bring forth):   waxing moon.

WEATHERWORKINGS (to quell):   waning moon.

WEIGHT GAIN: waxing moon.

WEIGHT LOSS: waning moon.

WISDOM (to increase):   waxing and full moons.

WISH-MAGICK: waxing and full moons.

The three Wiccan rituals that follow (Coven Empowerment, Cat Blessing, and Negativity Banishing) correspond respectively to the waxing, full, and waning phases of the moon. They are three examples of how the moon's changing cycle governs different types of magick.

An ancient lunar goddess. From *293 Renaissance Woodcuts for Artists and Illustrators*, (Dover Publications, Inc.)

COVEN EMPOWERING RITUAL

Perform this ritual on a night when the moon is in a waxing phase:

Two white candles are placed on the altar with a red candle (symbolizing energy) between them. An incense burner is also placed on the altar, along with whatever symbolic objects the coven traditionally employs to honor and represent the Old Ones (Goddess and God) and the four ancient elements.

All members of the coven gather, standing or seated on the floor in the form of a circle. Each person places a personal power-symbolizing object (such as an energy-charged crystal, a magickal pendant, a Goddess figurine, and so forth) upon a tray in the center of the circle.

The High Priestess of the coven casts the magick circle in a clockwise direction (also known as both sunrise and deosil), lights the candles and incense, and then says:

> WITH FLAME AND SMOKE THIS RITE BEGINS
> TO RAISE OUR POWER FROM WITHIN.
> ELEMENTAL SPIRITS OF OLD
> WE CALL THEE TO GUARD AND TO BEHOLD.

She joins the others in the circle. Everyone joins hands to form a human chain, and then the High Priestess says:

> HERE AND NOW WE JOIN AS ONE
> UNTIL OUR MAGICK DEEDS ARE DONE.
> POSITIVE ENERGY NOW PREVAILS,
> TO SHE WHO TURNS THE WHEEL WE HAIL!

All raise their arms up toward the sky, still holding hands, and say in unison:

> HAIL TO THE GODDESS!
> HAIL TO THE GODDESS!
> SHE IS OUR MOTHER
> SHE IS OUR TEACHER
> SHE IS WITHIN US
> AND ALL AROUND US.

All bring their arms back down to their original positions. Hands should remain joined together and sacred Goddess energy in the form of white light flowing from person to person clockwise around the circle should be visualized by all.

The High Priestess now says:

MAY THE ELEMENTALS
GUARD THIS CIRCLE,
GUIDE US INTO LIGHT
AND PROTECT US FROM THE DARK.
WITH HANDS TOUCHING HANDS
OUR SPIRITS UNITE;
ON A JOURNEY OF MAGICK
WE NOW EMBARK!

All members of the coven say in unison:

THE POWER OF THE GODDESS
IS WITHIN US!
THE POWER OF THE GOD
IS WITHIN US!

The High Priestess now says: THE POWER OF (she names something of power, such as THE EARTH, THE MOON, HEALING, the name of a favorite goddess or god, and so forth) IS WITHIN US!

The person to her left then says: THE POWER OF (she or he names something) IS WITHIN US!

As this is done, all should focus on the energy being raised and direct it toward the common goal.

The power-raising chant continues clockwise around the circle until all coven members have had three turns naming something to bring its power into the circle. (It is acceptable to name the same power source more than once if so desired.) The High Priestess now says:

WE ARE THE CHILDREN
OF THE WHITE LIGHT.
WE ARE ALL SISTERS AND
BROTHERS OF THE SACRED EARTH.
THE GODDESS AND THE GOD
ARE WITHIN US AND ALL AROUND US
AS WE FLOW WITH THE NEVER ENDING
CYCLE OF PERPETUAL REBIRTH.

All members of the coven say in unison:

LET THE FIRE OF OUR MAGICK
BURN BRIGHT AND BE STRONG;
LET OUR HEARTS HOLD THE POWER
TO RIGHT WHAT IS WRONG;
LET THE FORCES OF NATURE
BE AT OUR COMMAND;
LET THE POWER OF HEALING
BE HERE IN OUR HANDS.

The High Priestess now says:

ALL THINGS ARE POSSIBLE.
THE POWER OF CHANGE
AND TRANSFORMATION
IS ROOTED WITHIN EACH OF US
WAITING TO BLOSSOM LIKE A FLOWER,
NEEDING LOVE AND LIGHT

TO NOURISH ITS WONDROUS MAGICK.
LOVE IS THE LIGHT
AND LIGHT IS LOVE.

All members of the coven say in unison:

LOVE IS THE LIGHT
AND LIGHT IS LOVE
AND LOVE SHALL BE THE LAW:
AN' IT HARM NONE, LOVE
AND DO WHAT THOU WILT
SO MOTE IT BE!

The High Priestess should now proceed to uncast the circle in a counterclockwise (also known as widdershins) direction. As she does this she says:

TO THE ANCIENT ONES DIVINE
AND TO THE ELEMENTAL SPIRITS
OF AIR, FIRE, WATER, AND EARTH
WE LOVINGLY GIVE THANKS
FOR THY PRESENCE AND THY ENERGY
IN THIS TEMPLE OF MAGICK.
WITH THE DEEPEST RESPECT
AND HARMING NONE,
WE BID THEE FAREWELL.
THIS RITE IS NOW COMPLETE.
THIS CIRCLE IS NOW UNCAST.
BLESSED BE, ONE AND ALL.
SO MOTE IT BE!

All members of the coven say in unison:

SO MOTE IT BE!

CAT BLESSING

Perform this Wiccan ritual on a night when the moon is full and shining brightly, preferably the first night of the full moon at the exact moment when it enters into its full phase.

To find out the exact phase time, consult an up-to-date astrological or lunar calendar, book of days, or almanac. (I recommend either *Llewellyn's Magical Almanac* or the *Organic Gardening Almanac*, both published annually by Llewellyn Publications, St. Paul, Minnesota.)

If you desire, you may instead or also perform this ritual on your cat's birthday (if the date is known), on the anniversary of when he or she first became part of your family, or whenever you feel it to be the appropriate time.

Please note: This simple blessing can easily be adapted for dogs as well as your other furry friends and familiars.

(Stock Montage, Inc.)

Light some fragrant incense and place a gold candle (in honor of the Horned God) and a white candle (preferably one in the shape of a cat) on the center of your altar.

Cast a circle around your altar in whatever manner you usually cast it, and call upon the four elements of Air, Fire, Water, and Earth to be present and to serve as guardians of the circle.

Light the gold candle and then humbly invoke the powers of the Horned God:

O GREAT HORNED GOD
CONSORT OF THE GODDESS
I INVOKE THEE
AND INVITE THEE
INTO THIS CIRCLE.

Light the white cat candle and then, holding your cat gently in your arms, kneel before the altar and recite the following prayer:

O GREAT HORNED GOD,
FATHER OF THE WOODLANDS
AND LOVING LORD OF ALL CREATURES
THAT WALK, CRAWL, SWIM, AND FLY,
A THREEFOLD BLESSING I HUMBLY ASK
OF THEE ON THIS SPECIAL DAY:
MAY THIS CAT'S LIFE BE A LONG,
HAPPY, AND HEALTHY ONE;
MAY SHE (OR HE) ALWAYS RECEIVE
YOUR DIVINE PROTECTION;
AND WHEN OUR INCARNATIONS
IN THIS WORLD CEASE TO BE,
MAY WE FOREVER BE REUNITED

IN THE GREAT WICCAN OTHERWORLD
KNOWN ONLY AS SUMMERLAND.
SO MOTE IT BE!

After the prayer has been recited, gaze into the flame of the gold candle and chant thrice the name of your cat, each time followed by the words: BLESSED BE. Give the cat a loving kiss and place her or him down in the center of the circle. If the cat chooses to exit the circle at this point this is all right.

Give thanks to the Horned God in your own words and bid Him farewell. Next, give thanks to the four elements in your own words and then bid them farewell. Uncast the magick circle counterclockwise, and say:

IN PERFECT LOVE AND HARMING NONE
THIS PAGAN BLESSING NOW IS DONE.
SO MOTE IT BE!

Isadora (left) and Endora (right): two of the author's Calico familiars. (Photo by Gerina Dunwich)

NEGATIVITY BANISHING RITUAL

To banish all negative energies, perform this ritual on a night when the moon is in a waning phase.

This ritual may be performed by either a coven or a solitary practitioner of Wicca, and it can easily be adapted to suit the personal needs of the individual/s for whom it is being performed.

Place two white altar candles (or one silver and one gold) upon your altar to represent the Goddess and the Horned God. Between these candles place any type of black candle (taper or votive, scented or unscented). This candle will help to absorb the negative energies that are around and possibly within you, and transform them into positive ones.

Also on the altar, place a small cup of water and a small bowl containing salt (preferably sea salt) for consecration purposes, a cast-iron cauldron (or other fireproof pot), a stand for the cauldron (or a wooden cutting board to be placed underneath it to prevent it from scorching anything), rubbing alcohol, and matches.

Using an athame (a ritual knife), wand, sword, or besom (another name for a Witch's broom), cast a clockwise circle, and say:

BY THE MOTION OF THE SUN
THIS MAGICK CIRCLE I CREATE.
O ANCIENT ELEMENTS, ONE BY ONE
I SUMMON TO PARTICIPATE:
SPIRITS OF THE AIR,
GUARDIANS OF THE EAST;
SPIRITS OF THE FIRE,
GUARDIANS OF THE SOUTH;
SPIRITS OF THE WATER,
GUARDIANS OF THE WEST;

SPIRITS OF THE EARTH,
GUARDIANS OF THE NORTH.

Sprinkle a bit of water and salt around the sacred space you have just created, and say:

WITH WATER AND SALT I CONSECRATE
THIS SACRED TEMPLE OF MAGICK GREAT.

Light the white (or silver and gold) candles, and say:

I INVOKE THEE
O GREAT GODDESS,
MOTHER OF THE SILVER MOON,
I INVOKE THEE
O GREAT HORNED ONE,
FATHER OF THE GOLDEN SUN,
INTO THIS CIRCLE I INVITE
THY SACRED SHINING LIGHT
OF WHITE.

Visualize the circle around you glowing bright with divine energy in the form of white light. Let it surround you, and open yourself up to feel its loving, healing, negativity-banishing warmth.

Taking slow, deep breaths, visualize breathing the white light into your body and then breathing out all that is negative in the form of black smoke. Each time you inhale the white light and then exhale, see the black smoke grow less dark. Continue the white light breathing visualization technique until you feel completely cleansed of all inner negativity and you see only pure white light when you exhale.

Light the black candle, and say:

AS THE MOON WANES
AND GROWS DARKER,
SO SHALL ALL NEGATIVITY
GROW SMALLER AND SMALLER
UNTIL IT FADES AWAY
AND IS NO MORE.

LET LOVE BE THE POWER
TO BANISH ALL NEGATIVITY
SO THAT POSITIVE ENERGY
CAN ONCE AGAIN PREVAIL.

If needed, you may add additional requests to the prayer, such as:

LET LOVE BE THE POWER
TO OVERTURN BAD LUCK
AND BRING PROSPERITY
IN ALL ASPECTS OF LIFE.

LET LOVE BE THE POWER
TO HEAL ALL PAST REGRETS
AND TURN ALL SORROW
BACK INTO HAPPINESS.

LET LOVE BE THE POWER
TO TRANSFORM ALL FEELINGS
OF ANXIETY INTO PEACE OF MIND.

Pour a bit of the rubbing alcohol (about a quarter cup) into the cauldron. (WARNING: Be sure that the cauldron is resting on its stand or on a wooden cutting board, and is not near any flammable substances or things that can easily catch

(Photo by Gerina Dunwich)

on fire, such as drapes!) Light a match and drop it into the cauldron to make it flame.

Repeat the following magickal rhyme over and over until the fire in the cauldron burns itself completely out (which should take approximately three minutes):

ALL THAT IS BAD
NOW BE BANISHED!
ALL THAT IS NEGATIVE
NOW MUST VANISH!

Give thanks in your own words to the four spirits of the elements and then bid them farewell. Next, give thanks in your own words to the Goddess and the Horned God, and then bid them farewell.

Uncast the circle in a counterclockwise motion, and say:

THIS MAGICK RITE IS NOW COMPLETE.
THIS MAGICK CIRCLE IS NOW UNCAST.
SO MOTE IT BE!

Chapter 2

THE WHEEL
OF THE YEAR

There are eight religious holidays called Sabbats which are celebrated by most Wiccans throughout the course of a year. These Sabbats consist of the Spring and Autumn Equinoxes, the Summer and Winter Solstices, Candlemas, Beltane (also known as Walpurgisnacht), Lammas (also known as Lughansadh), and Samhain (also known as Halloween) which is perhaps the most important and widely celebrated Sabbat on the Witches' calendar.

These eight Sabbats make up the "spokes" of what is known as the Wheel of the Year. As each Sabbat is celebrated, so does the Wheel turn. It is constantly in motion, possessing neither beginning nor end. It is a perpetual cycle in complete harmony with the Earth and the magick of the four seasons, which most Pagans perceive as sacred gifts from Mother Nature and give thanks for. The Wheel is therefore

symbolic of the sun which rules over each changing season. It also represents the never-ending cycle of birth, death, and rebirth.

The Sabbats are known to be special times when solitary Witches and covens alike celebrate the changing seasons, pay homage to the Goddess and the Horned God, and perform magickal rites.

However, magick is not (and should not be) limited to just the eight seasonal celebrations of the Wheel. Every day of the year can be a time of magick, even if it is something as simple as the lighting of a candle followed by a Goddess-honoring prayer, a secret wish, or a divination of some kind. Keep in mind that the more positive magick we fill our lives with, the less negativity we will encounter, the closer we become to the Goddess and Her consort, and the more fine-tuned our powers become.

THE FOUR MAJOR SABBATS

CANDLEMAS SABBAT   (also known as Imbolc, Oimelc, and Lady Day) is celebrated annually on *February 2*. Traditional ritual herbs: angelica, basil, bay, benzoin, celandine, heather, myrrh, and all yellow flowers. Altar decorations traditionally include a crown of thirteen red candles, a sprig of evergreen, a besom or Witch's broom to symbolize the "sweeping out of the old," a small statue or figurine representing the Triple Goddess in Her aspect of the Maiden. Traditional Sabbat incense: basil, myrrh, and wisteria. Sacred Sabbat gemstones: amethyst, garnet, onyx, turquoise. Sabbat deities: The Goddess in Her Maiden aspect, Brigid (Celtic goddess of fire, wisdom, poetry, and sacred wells; also a deity associated with prophecy, divination, and the arts of healing), and Aradia (the daughter of Diana, and "founder of the Witch cult on Earth"). Candle colors: white, red, pink, brown. The Traditional Pagan foods of this Sabbat are those that represent growth, such as seeds (pumpkin, sesame, sunflower, etc.), poppyseed breads and cakes, and herbal teas.

BELTANE SABBAT   (also known as May Day, Rood Day, Rudemas, and Walpurgisnacht) is celebrated annually on May Eve and/or *May 1*. Traditional ritual herbs: almond, angelica, ash tree, bluebells, cinquefoil, daisy, frankincense, hawthorn, ivy, lilac, marigold, meadowsweet, primrose, roses, satyrion root, woodruff, and yellow cowslips. Altar decorations traditionally include a small Maypole and/or a phallus-shaped candle to symbolize fertility, a daisy chain, springtime wildflowers. Traditional Sabbat incense: frankincense, lilac, and rose. Sacred Sabbat gemstones: emerald, orange carnelian, sapphire, rose quartz. Sabbat deities: Flora (Roman flower-goddess), the lunar goddesses Diana and Artemis, Pan (the Greek horned goat-god of woodlands, fields, shepherds, and fertility), Faunus (the Roman equivalent to Pan), and all gods and goddesses who preside over fertility. Candle colors: dark green and all colors of the rainbow spectrum. The traditional Pagan foods of this Sabbat are all red fruits (such as strawberries and cherries), green herbal salads, red or pink wine punch, and large, round oatmeal or barley cakes known as "Beltane Cakes."

LAMMAS SABBAT (also known as Lughnasadh, August Eve, and the First Festival of Harvest) is celebrated annually on *August 1*. Traditional ritual herbs: acacia flowers, aloes, cornstalks, cyclamen, fenugreek, frankincense, heather, hollyhock, myrtle, oak leaves, sunflower, and wheat. Altar decorations traditionally include corn dollies (small figures fashioned from braided straw) and/or kirn babies (corncob dolls) to symbolize the Mother Goddess of the Harvest. Traditional Sabbat incense: aloes, rose, and sandalwood. Sacred Sabbat gemstones: aventurine, citrine, peridot, sardonyx. Sabbat deities: Lugh (a Celtic solar deity worshipped by the ancient Druids), John Barleycorn (the personification of malt liquor), Demeter, Ceres, the Corn Mother, and other goddesses who preside over agriculture. Candle colors: golden yellow, orange, green, light brown. The traditional Pagan foods of this Sabbat are homemade breads (wheat, oat, and especially corn bread), barley cakes, nuts, wild berries, apples, rice, roasted lamb, berry pies, elderberry wine, ale, and meadowsweet tea.

SAMHAIN SABBAT (also known as Halloween, Hallowmas, All Hallows' Eve, All Saints' Eve, Festival of the Dead, and the Third Festival of Harvest) is celebrated annually on *October 31*. Traditional ritual herbs: acorns, apples, broom, deadly nightshade, dittany, ferns, flax, fumitory, heather, mandrake, mullein, oak leaves, sage, and straw. Altar decorations traditionally include a jack-o'-lantern, apples, candles in the shapes of Witches, (as well as ghosts, black cats, skulls, etc.), photographs of deceased loved ones, tools of divination, a small statue or figure representing the Triple Goddess in Her aspect of the Crone. Traditional Sabbat incense: apple, heliotrope, mint, nutmeg, and sage. Sacred Sabbat gemstones: all black gemstones, especially jet, obsidian, and onyx. Sabbat deities: the Goddess in Her dark aspect of the Crone, Hecate (ancient Greek goddess of fertility and moon-magick, and the protectress of all Witches), Morrigan (the Celtic goddess who presides over death), Cernunnos (Celtic fertility god), and Osiris (an ancient Egyptian deity whose annual death and rebirth personified the self-renewing vitality and fertility of Nature). Candle colors: black and orange. The traditional Pagan foods of this Sabbat are apples, pumpkin pie, hazelnuts, Cakes for the Dead, corn, cranberry muffins and breads, ale, cider, and herbal teas (especially mugwort).

THE FOUR MINOR SABBATS

SPRING EQUINOX SABBAT (also known as Vernal Equinox Sabbat, Festival of the Trees, Alban Eilir, Ostara, and Rite of Eostre) is celebrated annually on *the first day of Spring*. Traditional ritual herbs: acorn, celandine, cinquefoil, crocus, daffodil, dogwood, Easter lily, honeysuckle, iris, jasmine, rose, strawberry, tansy, and violets. Altar decorations traditionally include hard-boiled eggs colored and painted with magickal symbols to symbolize fertility, a lucky rabbit's foot amulet, a bowl of green and yellow jellybeans. Sabbat incense: African violet, jasmine, rose, sage, and strawberry. Sacred Sabbat gemstones: amethyst, aquamarine, bloodstone, red jasper. Sabbat deities: Eostre (Saxon goddess of fertility), Ostara (German goddess of fertility), the Green Goddess, and Lord of the Greenwood. Candle colors: green, yellow, gold, and all pastel shades. The traditional Pagan foods of this Sabbat are hard-boiled eggs, honey cakes, the first fruits of the season, waffles, and milk punch.

SUMMER SOLSTICE SABBAT (also known as Midsummer, Alban Hefin, and Litha) is celebrated annually on *the first day of Summer*. Traditional ritual herbs: chamomile, cinquefoil, elder, fennel, hemp, larkspur, lavender, male fern, mugwort, pine, rose, Saint John's wort, wild thyme, wisteria, and verbena. Altar decorations traditionally include summertime flowers, love amulets, seashells, aromatic potpourri, Summer fruits. Traditional Sabbat incense: frankincense, lemon, myrrh, pine, rose, and wisteria. Sacred Sabbat gemstones: all green gemstones, especially emerald and jade. Sabbat deities: Aphrodite, Astarte, Freya, Hathor, Ishtar, Venus, and other goddesses who preside over love, passion, and beauty. Candle colors: blue, green, yellow. The traditional Pagan foods of this Sabbat are fresh vegetables, Summer fruits, pumpernickel bread, ale, and mead.

AUTUMN EQUINOX SABBAT (also known as the Fall Sabbat, Alban Elfed, and the Second Festival of Harvest) is celebrated annually on *the first day of Fall*. Traditional ritual herbs: acorns, asters, benzoin, ferns, honeysuckle, marigold, milkweed, mums, myrrh, oak leaves, passionflower, pine, rose, sage, Solomon's seal, and thistles. Altar decorations traditionally include acorns, pinecones, autumn leaves, a pomegranate (which symbolizes the goddess Persephone's descent into the Underworld), a small statue or figure representing the Triple Goddess in Her aspect of the Mother. Traditional Sabbat incense: benzoin, myrrh, and sage. Sacred Sabbat gemstones: carnelian, lapis lazuli, sapphire, yellow agate. Sabbat deities: The Goddess in Her Mother aspect, Persephone (Queen of the Underworld), and Thor (the Lord of Thunder in old Norse mythology). Candle colors: orange, dark red, yellow, indigo, brown. The traditional Pagan foods of this Sabbat are corn and wheat products, breads, nuts, vegetables, apples, roots (carrots, onions, potatoes, etc.), cider, and pomegranates.

WINTER SOLSTICE SABBAT (also known as Yule, Winter Rite, Midwinter, and Alban Arthan) is celebrated annually on *the first day of Winter*. Traditional ritual herbs: bay, bayberry, blessed thistle, cedar, chamomile, evergreen, frankincense, holly, juniper, mistletoe, moss, oak, pinecones, rosemary, and sage. Altar decorations traditionally include mistletoe, holly, a small Yule log, strings of colored lights, Yule/Christmas cards, a candle in the shape of Kriss Kringle (Santa Claus), presents wrapped in colorful holiday paper, a homemade wreath. Traditional Sabbat incense: bayberry, cedar, pine, and rosemary. Sacred Sabbat gemstones: cat's-eye and ruby. Sabbat deities: Lucina (Roman goddess of lunar mysteries), Frey (Scandinavian god of fertility and a deity associated with peace and prosperity), Attis (Phrygian fertility god), Dionysus (Greek god of wine), Woden (the chief Teutonic god), and, of course, jolly old Kriss Kringle (the Pagan god of Yule and personification of the Yuletide spirit).

Candle colors: red, green, white, gold, silver. The traditional Pagan foods of this Sabbat are roasted turkey, nuts, fruitcakes, caraway rolls, eggnog, and mulled wine.

SACRED GOD/DESS DAYS

Each day of the year is ruled by, and considered sacred to, one or more goddess and/or god from different Pagan cultures around the world.

To enhance the power of any magickal spells that call for the invocation of a particular deity, I strongly recommend that they be cast on that deity's corresponding day (or at any time during his or her sacred month, as the case may be). The same rule applies to any ritual performed in honor of, or to give thanks to, a particular goddess or god.

Below is an alphabetically arranged list of many Pagan deities, followed by their sacred times of the year:

A-MA (Portuguese goddess of fishermen): April 9

ADONIS (fertility/vegetation god and consort of Aphrodite): August 7

AEGIR (Teutonic god of the sea): March 3

AESTAS (Roman corn-goddess of summer): June 30

AHES: August 29

ALCYONE (Greek goddess): December 15

AMATERASU (Chinese sun goddess): July 17, December 8

AMAZON GODDESSES: April 9

ANAHIT (Armenian goddess of love): April 11

ANAHITA (Persian love goddess; also a deity associated with the Moon): August 2

ANAITIS (Persian goddess of the Moon): February 10

ANANTA (Indian serpent-goddess): August 31

ANDROS (the divine personification of manhood): November 30

ANNA (Roman goddess): June 18

ANTU (Babylonian creator goddess): the month of January

APET: the month of July

APHRODITE (Greek goddess of love): February 6 and the month of April

APOLLO (Greek god of light, healing, and hunting): April 16, May 25, and September 25

ARADIA (Daughter of Diana and first teacher of witchcraft to mankind): the month of February

ARANYA SASHTI (Indian god of woodlands): May 12

ARDVI (Persian goddess, mother of the stars): November 18

ARRIANRHOD (Celtic Mother-goddess): December 11

ARIES (god of battle): March 21

The Roman goddess Juno who was known to the ancient
Greeks as Hera.

ARTEMIS (Greek lunar-goddess, who also presided over wild
beasts and the art of hunting): the month of April, May
24, and December 29

ASTARTE: the months of April and November

ASTRAEA (Greek goddess of justice): December 8

ATHENA (Greek goddess of battle and patroness of the city of
Athens): March 19, May 20, the month of July, and September 21

ATTIS (Phrygian vegetation god): March 22, and the month
of December

AZAZEL (Hebrew): September 26

BAAL (Phoenician solar deity):   October 28
BABO: January 8
BACCHUS (god of wine and mirth-making):   November 11
BALOMAIN (Kalish demi-god):   December 23
BAU (Babylonian goddess and the mother of Ea):   April 10
BENDI (lunar goddess of the Balkan Peninsula):   June 6
BERTHA (German goddess):   January 1
BETORO BROMO (Indonesian god of fire):   January 16
BLACK MADONNA: December 12
BLAJINI (Rumanian spirt-gods of both water and the under-
   world):   April 7
BONA DEA (the Good Goddess):   May 3 and December 3
BRIGIT (Celtic earth-mother and goddess of fire, wisdom,
   poetry, and sacred wells):   February 1
BRUMA (Roman goddess of the Winter season):   December 11
CAILLEACH (Celtic Crone-goddess):   November 1
CAPROTINA (goddess of the fig tree):   July 7
CARMAN (goddess of poetry):   September 23
CARMENTA (Roman nymph of prophesy):   January 11
CARNA (Roman goddess of doors and locks):   June 1
CARPO (goddess of Autumn):   September 23
CASTOR AND POLLUX (sons of Greek god Zeus):   October 25
CATHERINE (Queen of the Shades):   November 25
CEADDA (god of healing springs and sacred wells):   March 2
CERES (Roman goddess of the fruitful Earth):   January 30,
   February 1, February 28, April 12, May 29, the month of
   August, and October 4
CERNUNNOS (horned god):   October 18
CERRIDWEN (Celtic goddess of fertility):   June 20
CHANGING WOMAN (Native American, Apache tribe):   Septem-
   ber 4
CHANGO (Yoruban god of lightning bolts):   December 4

➤ 33

CHICOMECOATL (Aztec): June 30

CHU-SI-NIU (Taiwanese goddess who presides over the birth of mortals): April 12

COATLIQUE (Aztec mother goddess): December 12

CONSUS (Roman god of the harvest): August 27

COPPER WOMAN (Native American): July 18

CORN MOTHER: the month of August

CYBELE (the Great Mother): March 24, April 4, and December 3

DAENA (Maiden goddess of the Parsees): September 7

DEA DIA (goddess of the cosmos): May 17

DEER MOTHER (Native American spirit goddess): January 3

DEMETER (Greek vegetation and mother goddess): February 28, the month of August, September 17, September 28, and December 7

DEVAKI (ancient Indian Mother-goddess): August 27

DIANA: April 11, May 27, and August 17

DIEV (Latvian god): December 18

DIKAIOSUNE (ancient Pagan god who presided over justice): July 12

DIONYSUS (Greek god of wine): January 3, March 19, July 9, September 2, October 5, and the month of December

DOMHNACH CHROM DUBH (Irish sacrificial god): July 28

DOMNA (Irish goddess of sacred stones): June 5

DURGA (Mother goddess): October 14

EGYPTIAN THREEFOLD GODDESS (the Mother, the Daughter, and the Dark Mother): September 21

EINHERJAR (spiritual warriors who protect the gods): November 11

EKEKO (Aymara Indian god of prosperity): January 24

ELENA (Helen, goddess of the holy road): May 2

ELIHINO (Cherokee Earth goddess): August 6

EOSTRE (Saxon fertility goddess):   the first day of spring
EPONA (Celtic Mother goddess and the patroness of horses):
   December 18
ERZULIE FREDA (voodoo goddess of love):   July 16
EURYDICE (Greek type nymph/underworld goddess):   June 17
FAUNUS: the month of May
FELICITAS (Roman goddess of good fortune):   the month of
   January and October 9
FERONA (ancient goddess of fire, fertility, and woodlands):
   November 15
FIDES (Roman goddess who personified faithfulness):   October 1
FLORA (Roman goddess of flowers):   April 28, and May 23
FORTUNA (Roman goddess of good fortune):   June 24
FORTUNA REDUX (Roman goddess of journeys and safe returns):
   October 12
FREYA (Norse goddess of fertility, love, and beauty):   January 8
   and December 27
FRIGG (the chief goddess of old England):   January 12
FUJI (Japanese goddess of fire):   July 1
FURRINA (ancient Italian goddess of springs):   July 25
GAIA (Mother Earth):   February 28
GANESH (Hindu elephant god of good luck and prosperity):
   September 5
GAURI (Indian goddess of marriage):   March 27
GE (Ancient Earth goddess):   February 28
GLOOSCA (the father god, Micmac Indian tribe):   July 30
GOD OF THE SUMMER SUN (Native American, Plains tribe):
   June 27
GRANNY MARCH (Bulgarian Witch goddess):   March 1
GREEN GODDESS (Pagan goddess of springtime, nature, and fer-
   tility):   the month of March
GREEN MAN (ancient Pagan fertility god):   June 23

GUJESWARI (Indian Mother Goddess): November 27

GULA (Babylonian goddess of birth): September 19 and October 24

GWYNN AP NUDD (Celtic god of the underworld and the faerie kingdom): September 29

HATHOR (Egyptian cow-headed goddess): January 23, August 7, and the month of November

HAWK MAIDEN (Native American, Hopi tribe): December 16

HECATE (Greek moon-goddess, Crone, and the protectress of all Witches): August 13 and November 7

HEIMDALL (Norse god): September 29

HEMERA (Greek goddess of day): June 28

HERA (Consort of the Greek god Zeus): June 19

HERCULES (Heroic Greek god known for his extraordinary strength): August 21

HERMES TRISMESTIGUS (the patron of alchemists): May 24

HETTSUI NO KAMI (Japanese kitchen-range goddess): November 8

HOGMAGOG (Scottish god of the sun): December 31

HOLDA: July 10

HOLIKA (Indian demon-goddess): March 16

THE HORAE (Three Greek goddesses who presided over the changing seasons): September 25

HORNED GOD (Wiccan): May 8

HORUS (Egyptian sky god): July 14

IA: February 5

IDUNA (Norse goddess): March 20

IGAEHINDVO (goddess of the Sun, Elihino's sister): August 6

ILMATER (Finnish water Mother): August 26

INANNA (Sumerian Queen of Heaven): January 2

ING (hearth-god): May 14

INVICTI SOLIS (ancient Roman solar deity, the Invisible Sun): December 25

IRENE (Daughter of Jupiter and Themis and one of the Horae): January 29

IRISH LUNANTISHEES (spirit guardians of the blackthorn tree): November 11

ISHTAR (Babylonian goddess of love and war): January 27, March 29, and June 2

ISIS (Egyptian mother goddess): January 2, March 20, July 19, and August 12

JAGANNATH (benevolent incarnation of the Indian god Vishnu): June 14

JANUS (Roman double-faced god of passage): the month of January, especially January 1

JUNO: May 29, the month of June, and July 8

JUNO FEBRUA: the month of February

JUNO-LUPA (Roman she-wolf goddess): February 14

JUSTICIA (Roman goddess of justice): January 8

JUTURNO (Italian goddess of springs and wells): January 11

KACHINAS (Native American, Hopi tribe): July 26

KALI (Hindu destroyer goddess): February 17 and the month of November

KRISHNA (The eighth incarnation of the Hindu god Vishnu): August 27

KONHANA-HIME (Japanese granddaughter-goddess of Amaterasu): November 23

KRONOS (Father Time): July 11

KUAN YIN (Chinese goddess of healing and mercy): January 31, March 28, and April 5

KUKULCAN (Mayan god): November 21

KUPALA (Russian fertility goddess): June 21

LAKSHMI (one of the Three Mothers, along with Parvati and Sarasvati): March 20 and October 16

LARA (Roman earth mother goddess): December 23

LARES (Roman household gods): January 12

An Eighth-century sculpture of the Hindu god Vishnu. (British Museum London)

LAURENTINA (Roman mother of the Lares):   December 23
LIBER PATER (Roman god of wine):   March 27
LIBERTAS (Roman goddess of liberty):   April 13
LIBERTY (goddess of freedom):   December 10
LOKI (Norse trickster god):   April 1
LONO (Hawaiian god):   November 7
LORD OF THE GREENWOOD (Pagan fertility god of English origin similar to Pan):   the month of March

LUCINA (Pagan goddess of light who was later Christianized into Saint Lucia):   December 5

LUGH (Celtic solar deity):   July 31 and the month of August

LUNA (Roman goddess of the Moon):   March 31

LUNA REGIA (Gnostic lunar goddess):   April 24

LU PAN (Chinese patron of carpenters):   July 18

LUPERCUS (Roman god of wolves):   February 15

LUTZELFRAU AND PERCHTA (German Yuletide Witches):   December 25

MAAT (Egyptian goddess of wisdom and inner truth):   July 5 and December 16

MACHENDRANA (Himalayan rain god):   April 17

MAIA (Roman goddess of Springtime):   May 1

MAIDENS OF THE FOUR DIRECTIONS (Hopi tribe):   September 3

MAMAN: the month of November

MANES (Greek spirits of the underworld):   November 8

MARS (Roman god of battle):   March 23, May 29, and October 15

MARYAMMA (or Mariamne):   April 14

MEDITRINA (Roman goddess of medicine and healing):   September 30

MENS (Roman goddess of the mind):   June 8

MINERVA (Roman goddess of battle):   February 19, June 14, October 24, and December 4

MOCCAS (Celtic fig tree goddess):   November 14

MOON HARE (Chinese lunar diety):   September 27

MORRIGAN (Celtic goddess of war, fertility, and vegetation):   the month of October and December 16

MOTHER OF THE UNIVERSE (Indian Triple Goddess whose three aspects are Sarasvati, Lakshmi, and Parvati):   November 27

NAGAS (Snake-gods of Nepal):   July 1

NEITH (ancient Egyptian Earth-goddess of the Delta):   December 8

NEMESIS (Greek goddess of fate): August 23
NEPHTHYS (goddess of death): July 18 and September 13
NEPTUNE (god of the sea): July 23
NINCNEVIN (Scottish goddess): November 10
NINA (An aspect of the Sumerian mother goddess Inanna): February 19
NU KWA (Chinese goddess of healing): August 22
OBATALA (Yoruban hermaphrodite deity): September 24
ODDUDUA (Santerian Mother-goddess): August 11
. OLD LADY OF THE ELDER TREES (Germany and Denmark): October 11
OLD WOMAN (Lithuanian corn goddess): October 5
OPS (Roman goddess of sowing and reaping): August 25 and December 19
OSIRIS (brother and consort of the Egyptian goddess Isis): July 13, September 24, the month of October, and November 3
OSTARA (German fertility goddess): the first day of Spring
PALES (Roman pastoral deity): April 21
PAN (Grecco-Roman satyr god of shepherds and huntsmen): the month of May
PANDROSOS (Greek goddess): October 18
PAPA LEGBA (Voodoo god of the crossroads): June 29
PARVATI (one of the Three Mothers along with Lakshmi and Sarasvati): March 20
PAX (Roman goddess of peace): January 29 and July 4
PERCHTA (German witch goddess of the yule-tide season): December 25
PERSEPHONE: April 3 and the first day of Autumn
POMONA: November 1
PROSERPINA: May 27
PRYTANIA (Britannia): March 24
PUCK (Robin Goodfellow): August 11
PYTHON (Greek serpent goddess): May 28

A coven of Witches dancing around the satyr-like Horned God, who presides over nature, wild animals, fertility, and the dark half of the year.

QUETZALCOATL (Aztec fertility god): September 20 and November 21

RAMA (Hindu god): April 18

REASON (French goddess): November 10

RHEA (Greek Earth goddess): July 11 and December 3

RHIANNON (Celtic/Welsh Mother goddess): March 4

ROWANA (or Rauni, goddess of the sacred rowan tree): July 15

SALAVI (Native American spruce tree/rain god): June 26

SANKRANT (Hindu goddess): December 19

SARASVATI (one of the Three Mothers, along with Lakshmi and Parvati): January 31, March 20, and November 27

SATURN (Roman astral god identified with the planet Saturn): March 23 and December 17 through 24

SEDNA (Eskimo goddess of both the sea and the underworld): September 25

SEKHMET (Egyptian cow goddess): January 7, the month of November

SET (Egyptian god of darkness and the magickal arts): July 15

SEVEN SHINTO GODS OF GOOD LUCK (Japanese): October 19

SHEELA-NA-GIG (Irish fertility goddess): March 18

SHIVA (Hindu god of destruction and renewal): February 24 and May 10

SITALA (Indian goddess): March 19

SKADI (European goddess of the underworld): July 10, November 30

SNOW QUEEN GODDESS (A northern goddess who presides over the winter season): December 11

SOPHIA (or Sapientia, goddess of wisdom): October 24, November 28, and December 16

SOTHIS (Egyptian astral goddess and personification of the star Sirius): the month of July

SPANDARMAT (Persian goddess): February 18

SPIDER WOMAN (Native American, Hopi tribe): the month of July and December 16

SULIS (goddess of hot springs): July 23

SUNNA (Norse goddess of the Sun): July 8

SURYA (Indian god of the Sun): January 14 through 16

TACITA (Roman goddess of silence): February 18

TARA (Hindu goddess whose name means star): October 31

TARI PENNU (Indian Earth goddess): August 30

TEINNE (or Tan, Celtic personification of holy fire): August 6

TELLUS MATER (Mother Earth): January 30

TEMPESTAS (powerful ancient goddess who controlled storms): June 1

TERMINUS (Roman god of boundaries): February 23

TERRA (Consort of Uranus and one of the most ancient deities in mythology): the month of April

THESEUS (deified Greek hero): September 26

THOR (Norse god of thunder and lightning): January 19, July 28, and the month of September

THOTH (Egyptian god of both wisdom and the magickal arts): September 19

THREE FATES (The three Greek goddesses Atropos, Klotho, and Lachesis, who presided over the course of human life): May 27

THREEFOLD GODDESS (Wicca): November 16

TIAMAT (Babylonian Dragon-Mother): November 6

TIN HAU (Chinese goddess of the North Star): May 10

TI-TSANG (Chinese god of the underworld): July 15

TIU (an ancient Teutonic chief god and ruler of the year): January 13

TONANTZIN (Guadualupe goddess of mercy): December 9 through 12

TYI WARA (African god of agriculture): April 27

TYR (Anglo-Saxon god of the battlefield): October 17

UA ZIT (Egyptian serpent goddess): March 14

URSALA (Slavic goddess of the moon): October 21

ULLR (god of Wintertime and archery): November 22

VALI (Norse archer god): February 14

VENUS (Roman goddess of love): the months of January and April, and August 8

VERTUMNUS (Roman god of the changing seasons): August 23

VESTA (goddess of the hearth): January 15, March 1, June 7 through 15, and August 15

VICTORIA (Roman goddess personifying success and triumph): October 7

VIDAR (son of Norse god Odin): June 14

VISHNU (Hindu creator god who appears as ten major incarnations): October 6 through 15

VULCAN (Roman god of volcanic eruptions): August 23

WALPURGA (Saxon goddess after whom the Walpurgisnacht sabbat is named):   April 30

WITCH OF GAETA (Italian witch Goddess):   July 3

WODEN: the month of December

XIPE TOTEC (Mexican god of death):   October 30

YAMA (Buddhist god of death and the underworld):   July 12

YING-HUA: the month of April

YNGONA (Danish goddess):   January 21

YSAHODHARA (corsort of Buddha):   May 2

YUKI ONNE: December 11

ZAMYAZ (ancient Persian deity):   February 28

ZAO JUN (Chinese kitchen god):   January 18

ZEUS (the most powerful of Greek gods):   June 12

A wheel of the twelve signs of the Zodiac surrounding the deities Mercury, Jupiter, Venus, and Amor.

Chapter 3

THE RAINBOW
OF MAGICK

I call this section "The Rainbow of Magick" because, just as a rainbow is made up of many different colors, so too is the Wiccan art of spellcraft.

Colors possess various meanings and powers, and are an important aspect of magick. For instance, whenever you cast a spell (no matter how simple or elaborate it may be, or for whatever purpose you have in mind), it is a good idea to always involve at least one candle that is of a color corresponding to the correct energy vibrations and influences. This will enable you to focus more clearly, tune into the right energies, and attain not only positive results, but powerful ones as well.

Pagan goddesses and gods each have their own colors that are sacred to them. Therefore, when honoring or invoking them in rituals, it is only polite to use a candle that corresponds correctly to their color (or colors, as some have more than one).

Color is also used for healing the body, the mind, and also the spirit. The method used is most commonly known as "color visualization" and it is practiced by many modern Witches, Pagans, and New Agers the world over.

It is usually performed by lighting a candle of the appropriate color (see below), entering a meditative state in order to connect with the Goddess and Horned God, and then visualizing the aura of the person in need of healing to be completely surrounded by a light of the proper healing color (see below). This color is focused in on any specific areas of pain or illness for at least an hour, changed to white (or transparent), and then withdrawn in a slow manner.

As aura colors are visualized for healings, the actual aura colors are read and interpreted by those who possess the special gift of aura-sight (the psychic ability to perceive auras which are normally invisible to the naked human eye). The different colors, as well as color combinations, that appear all possess different meanings which are discussed below.

The reading of auras is not an ability that all people, even Wiccans, readily possess. Of course, as with most talents (psychic and otherwise), some people are naturally more adept than others when it comes to working with auras.

All things in nature (including humans, animals, plants, and even minerals) radiate an aura of some type; however, these "envelopes of energy" as they are often called are not visible to the average naked eye. Those who see auras are usually born with the skill (which is often passed down from generation to generation and first becomes apparent in early childhood). Some persons develop it through accidental means (such as through head injuries or being struck by lightning), and some are able to fine-tune their aura-reading abilities by meditating and performing various psychic exercises as part of their daily routine.

However, the aura work that this chapter of the book is concerned with requires no special clairvoyant talents, only the simple ability to *visualize,* which nearly anyone can do with a little bit of practice and patience. To perform an aura healing, you need only to use your imagination to project the image of an aura of the appropriate healing color around the person, animal, or plant you are working on.

For instance, if you are suffering from a headache, to cure it you should sit comfortably and peacefully, gazing into a mirror, and use the power of your own mind to visualize a healing green aura radiating from your head like a halo. Clear your mind of all distracting thoughts and concentrate only upon the aura. If your powers of visualization are strong and you have enough faith in your own inner powers, your headache should vanish within a very short time.

The following is a list of colors (arranged alphabetically), followed by their magickal correspondences and healing properties (if any), the various Pagan deities to whom they are sacred, and an example of how many colors are interpreted by some diviners of auramancy (the art and practice of divination by auras):

BLACK   is the appropriate color for candles used in uncrossing rituals and spells designed to banish negativity or conjure spirits of the dead. Black is the traditional color used in necromantic divination.

As a visualization color, black is generally not considered one that possesses any significant healing properties.

It is a color sacred to the Pagan deities Anu, Anubis, Ereshkigal, Exu, Freya, Hades, Hecate, Hera, Kali, Morrigan, Nyx, Odin, Osiris, Persephone, Set, Thanatos, Thunor, the Triple Goddess in Her Crone aspect, and all deities who rule the Underworld and all things dark.

BLUE   is the appropriate color for candles used in the following types of magick: astral projection, spells and rituals that involve honor, loyalty, peace, tranquillity, truth, and wisdom. Burn blue candles for protection during sleep (especially against nightmares, incubus or succubus demons, and psychic attack). They can also assist in inducing dreams of a prophetic nature when anointed with oil containing powdered mugwort, and burned prior to bedtime.

As a healing visualization color, blue soothes and relaxes. It is excellent for treating such ailments as burns, diarrhea, fever, headaches, high blood pressure, insomnia, menstrual pain, rheumatism, skin rashes, sore throat, sunburn, ulcers, and minor wounds.

It is a color sacred to the Pagan deities Aditi, Chloris, Dyaus, Ea, Hathor, Horus (royal blue), Neptune, Nut (royal blue), Poseidon (light blue), Tane, Thor (dark blue), Thunor (dark blue), Tiwaz, Uranus, and Xochiquetzal.

An aura that appears blue or blue combined with green indicates good health and/or the overcoming of personal karmic patterns from previous incarnations.

BROWN   is the appropriate color for candles used in spells to find misplaced objects and improve the powers of concentration and telepathy. Spells involving persons born under the astrological sign of Capricorn will be more potent if brown candles are used. These are also the candle colors traditionally used by many modern Witches in spells and rituals designed for protection of familiars and household pets.

Brown is a color sacred to the Pagan deities Ceres, Daghda, Frija, Hera (dark brown), Ninhursag (dark brown), Parvati, and Tlazolteotl.

GOLD   is the appropriate color for candles used in the following types of magick: spells that attract the power of cosmic influences and rituals performed in honor of solar deities.

It is a color sacred to the Pagan deities Amaterasu, Apollo, Balder, Dazhbog, Lugh, Ra, and Zeus.

An aura that appears as light gold-colored indicates a spiritual and highly evolved soul that has lived many lifetimes and is now in its final incarnation on this plane of existence.

GRAY   is the appropriate color for candles in spells to neutralize negative influences.

As a visualization color, gray is generally not used as it possesses no significant healing properties.

It is perhaps the least favorable color to be seen in an aura reading, for gray auras usually emanate from persons who are in the final stages of a terminal illness or those who are destined to soon die by accident, suicide, or at the hands of another.

GREEN   is the appropriate color for candles used in the following types of magick: spells involving fertility, success, good luck, prosperity, money matters, rejuvenation and ambition, rituals to counteract greed and jealousy, and spells involving persons born under the astrological sign of Taurus.

As a healing visualization color, green is excellent for treating boils, cancers, colds, headaches, high blood pressure, kidney ailments, nervousness, and ulcers.

It is a color sacred to the Pagan deities Amon, Anaitis, Arrianrhod, Asherali, Astarte, Attis, Baal, Ceara, Centeotle, Cernunnos (dark green), Cerridwen, Cybele, Daghda, Demeter, Dew, Dionysus, Eostre, Esmeralda, Faunus, Frey, Ishtar, Isis, Kuan Yin, Lupercus, Mut, Mylitta, Pan, Pomona, Sylvanus (dark green), Tane, Tlazolteotl, the Triple Goddess in Her Mother aspect, and Yarilo.

When the color green or green combined with blue is observed in a person's aura, it is said to be an indication of

good health and the overcoming of personal karmic patterns
from past lives.

ORANGE   is the appropriate color for candles used in spells to
stimulate energy.

As a healing visualization color, orange is stimulating and
energizing. It possesses a number of the same properties as the
color red and is ideal for treating such ailments as arthritis,
asthma, bronchitis, constipation, coughs, depression, epilepsy,
and exhaustion.

It is a color sacred to the Pagan deities Dazhbog (orange-
red), Demeter, Pele, and Saturn.

An aura that appears orange-colored indicates the presence
of confusion as well as a constantly changing nature.

PINK   is the appropriate color for candles used in love spells
and rituals involving friendship and youthful femininity.

As a healing visualization color, pink (specifically rose) protects, rejuvenates, and brings hope, restful sleep, and pleasant
dreams. Rose is excellent for treating ailments of the heart,
anxiety, constipation, depression, hearing loss, and kidney
problems. It is also good for those who suffer from nightmares
and sleep disorders.

It is a color sacred to the Pagan deities Aphrodite, Benten,
and Venus.

PURPLE   is the appropriate color for candles used in the following types of magick: psychic manifestations, healings, and
spells involving power, success, independence, and household
protection.

It is a color sacred to the Pagan deities Athena, Bacchus,
Dionysus, Odin, Thoth, and Woden.

As a healing visualization color, the lighter shades of purple (violet in particular) are highly spiritual and inspirational.

They aid in meditation, psychic development and creativity, and are excellent for treating such ailments as allergies, asthma, baldness, blood clots, colds, gout, mental disorders, sinus problems, sleep disorders, stress-related diseases, and tumors.

When the color purple is present in an aura, it indicates that a material and/or spiritual healing is taking place. If a person's aura is a light shade of purple or lavender, it indicates that he or she possesses the natural ability to heal others. (This ability may or may not be known to the person at the time of the aura reading.)

RED is the appropriate color for candles used in the following types of magick: fertility rites, aphrodisiacs, and spells involving sexual passion, love, health, physical strength, revenge, anger, willpower, courage, and magnetism. Spells involving persons born under the astrological sign of Aries or Scorpio will be more potent if red candles are used.

As a healing visualization color, red symbolizes energy and life. It is a fiery, invigorating color which is recommended for treating such ailments as anemia, cancer, exhaustion, frostbite, leukemia, liver infections, neuralgia, and paralysis.

It is a color sacred to the Pagan deities Angi, Aodh, Aphrodite, Astarte, Cearas, Chernobog, Chu-Jung, Durga, Eros, Freya, Hestia, Inanna, Ishtar, Kupala, Loki, Morrigan (scarlet), Nemesis, Odin, Pele, Sekhmet (crimson), Vesta, and Woden.

A completely red aura is believed to indicate an individual's deteriorating health or the presence of disease. The brighter the shade of red appears in an aura, the greater the likelihood of serious health problems.

SILVER is the appropriate color for candles used in spells and rituals to remove negativity, encourage stability, and attract the influence of the Goddess. Lunar spellwork and magick involving persons born under the astrological sign of Gemini or Cancer also call for silver candles.

The color silver is sacred to the Pagan deities Artemis, Asherali, Diana, Fortuna, Hecate, Luna, Selene, Svarog, and Thoth.

WHITE is the appropriate color for candles used in the following types of magick: consecration rituals, meditation work, divinations, exorcisms, and spells dealing with all forms of healing, clairvoyance, truth, peace, spiritual strength, and lunar energy.

As a healing visualization color, white symbolizes innocence, purity, and peace. It is an excellent color to use for astral travel, crystal gazing, inner peace, meditation, and summoning spirit guides. The color white helps to prevent stroke, increases breast milk in nursing women, and is ideal for treating such ailments as broken bones, calcium deficiency, and pain caused by problems of the teeth.

It is a color sacred to the Pagan deities Anu, Apollo, Arrianrhod, Artemis, Asherali, Astraea, Athena, Bast, Brigit, Chloris, Diana, Epona, Exu, Flora, Frigga, Janus, Khons, Kilya, Lucina, Luna, Maat, Min, Parvati, Ptah, Rhiannon, Selene, Sin, and the Triple Goddess in Her aspect of the Maiden (or Virgin).

A white aura, like a gold-colored one, indicates a spiritual and highly evolved soul that has lived many lifetimes and is now in its final incarnation on this plane of existence.

YELLOW is the appropriate color for candles used in spells that involve attraction, charm, confidence, and persuasion. Like gold, it can also serve for magick and rituals involving solar energies, and deities associated with the sun. Spells involving persons born under the astrological sign of Gemini or Leo are more potent when yellow candles are used.

As a healing visualization color, yellow is stimulating and uplifting. It helps to dispel all types of fears and is an ideal color to use for treating such ailments as constipation, diabetes, heartburn, indigestion, menstrual cramps, and most skin conditions.

It is a color sacred to the Pagan deities Amaterasu, Balder, Ceres, Dazhbog, Lugh, and Shamash.

A yellow aura indicates freedom of self expression, and affirmative answers to specific problems facing the person with the aura. However, yellow combined with red indicates confusion and a constantly changing nature.

THE RAINBOW CANDLE SPELL

The following is what one might call a "multipurpose" spell which can be performed during any month of the year as needed. When carried out correctly, it helps banish all things of a negative nature and strengthens all positive virtues, as well as pays homage to both the Goddess and Her consort, the Horned God.

To perform this spell, you will need an athame, candle anointing oil (preferably myrrh oil), a book of matches or a lighter, and thirteen votive-size candles (one each of the following colors: black, blue, brown, gold, gray, green, orange, pink, purple, red, silver, white, and yellow).

On a night when the moon is almost full but still in its waxing phase, cast a circle to establish a sacred space in which to perform this spell. Unless you have your own special method of circle-casting, I recommend doing it in the following manner:

Using an athame or wand and beginning in the direction of east, trace a clockwise (also known as sunwise) circle on the ground. As you do this, say:

SUNWISE WITH A WITCHES' BLADE
THIS SACRED CIRCLE NOW IS MADE.
ELEMENTAL SPIRITS OF OLD
I CALL THEE TO GUARD
AND TO BEHOLD.

If you are working with a coven, you may add the following lines to the circle-casting incantation:

HERE AND NOW WE JOIN AS ONE
UNTIL OUR MAGICK DEEDS ARE DONE.

Arrange the thirteen candles in the shape of a rainbow on the center of your altar, starting from the left with the silver candle, followed by the gold, white, gray, black, orange, yellow, purple, red, blue, brown, green, and pink one.

If you do not have an altar, you may place the candles in a rainbow shape before you on the floor in the center of the circle and perform the spell while kneeling or sitting cross-legged on a pillow.

It is also a good idea to use some type of fireproof holder for each candle.

Repeat the following words as you anoint each candle with a few drops of the myrrh oil:

I CONSECRATE THEE
AS A TOOL TO MAGICK
AND I CHARGE THEE WITH POWER
IN THE NAME OF THE GODDESS
AND IN THE NAME OF THE GOD.
SO MOTE IT BE!

After all thirteen candles have been anointed, light the silver one first, and say:

O CANDLE OF SILVER
I GIVE THEE FLAME
IN HONOR OF THE GODDESS
AND THE WAXING MOON ABOVE.
MAY THEY BLESS AND PROTECT
OUR CIRCLE AND THE MAGICK
THAT WITHIN IT THIS NIGHT
SHALL BE BROUGHT TO LIFE.
SO MOTE IT BE!

Light the gold candle next, and say:

O CANDLE OF GOLD
I GIVE THEE FLAME
IN HONOR OF THE HORNED GOD
WHO IS KNOWN BY MANY NAMES.
MAY HE BLESS AND PROTECT
OUR CIRCLE AND THE MAGICK
THAT WITHIN IT THIS NIGHT
SHALL BE BROUGHT TO LIFE.
SO MOTE IT BE!

Light the white candle next, and say:

O CANDLE OF WHITE
I GIVE THEE FLAME
FOR IN YOUR LIGHT THERE IS TRUTH,
PURITY AND SPIRITUAL STRENGTH.
AS YOU BURN BRIGHT AND STRONG
MAY I LEARN TO BE MORE CENTERED
AND MAY I BE BLESSED WITH WHOLENESS.
SO MOTE IT BE!

Light the gray candle next, and say:

O CANDLE OF GRAY
I GIVE THEE FLAME
SO THAT ALL NEGATIVE ENERGY
FROM WITHIN AND WITHOUT
MAY NOW BE NEUTRALIZED.
SO MOTE IT BE!

Light the black candle next, and say:

O CANDLE OF BLACK
I GIVE THEE FLAME
SO THAT ALL EVIL
MAY NOW BE BANISHED
AND ALL SORROW AND DISCORD
BE BROUGHT TO A CLOSE.
BLESS ME WITH THE POWER
TO LET GO OF THE PAST
AND PUT TO REST THAT
WHICH IS NO LONGER
SO THAT FROM THIS ENDING
A NEW BEGINNING CAN EMERGE.
SO MOTE IT BE!

Light the orange candle next, and say:

O CANDLE OF ORANGE
I GIVE THEE FLAME
FOR IN YOUR LIGHT THERE IS
ENCOURAGEMENT AND STIMULATION,
ADAPTATION AND ORGANIZATION.
AS YOU BURN BRIGHT AND STRONG

MAY MY POWERS OF SELF-CONTROL
AND CONCENTRATION BE STRENGTHENED.
SO MOTE IT BE!

Light the yellow candle next, and say:

O CANDLE OF YELLOW
I GIVE THEE FLAME
FOR IN YOUR LIGHT THERE IS UNITY,
PERSUASION, AND CREATIVITY.
AS YOU BURN BRIGHT AND STRONG
MAY MY CONFIDENCE BE INCREASED
AND MY MIND POWER BE STRENGTHENED.
SO MOTE IT BE!

Light the purple candle next, and say:

O CANDLE OF PURPLE
I GIVE THEE FLAME
FOR IN YOUR LIGHT THERE IS
AMBITION, DIGNITY, AND INDEPENDENCE.
BLESS ME WITH WISDOM,
BLESS ME WITH PROTECTION.
AS YOU BURN BRIGHT AND STRONG
MAY MY PSYCHIC AND OCCULT POWERS
ALSO GROW IN STRENGTH.
SO MOTE IT BE!

Light the red candle next, and say:

O CANDLE OF RED
I GIVE THEE FLAME
FOR IN YOUR LIGHT THERE IS

STRENGTH, ENERGY, AND PASSION.
BLESS ME WITH WILL POWER,
BLESS ME WITH COURAGE.
LIKE THE BLOOD OF LIFE
WHICH FLOWS THROUGH MY VEINS
MAY YOUR FORCE ALWAYS FLOW
THROUGHOUT MY BODY, MY MIND,
AND MY SPIRITUAL SELF.
SO MOTE IT BE!

Light the blue candle next, and say:

O CANDLE OF BLUE
I GIVE THEE FLAME
FOR IN YOUR LIGHT THERE IS
PEACE, INSPIRATION, AND TRANQUILITY.
AS YOU BURN BRIGHT AND STRONG
MAY I COME TO KNOW THE VIRTUES OF
PATIENCE, LOYALTY, AND UNDERSTANDING.
SO MOTE IT BE!

Light the brown candle next, and say:

O CANDLE OF BROWN
I GIVE THEE FLAME
FOR IN YOUR LIGHT THERE IS
STABILITY AND EARTHINESS.
AS YOU BURN BRIGHT AND STRONG
MAY I LEARN TO OVERCOME
INDECISION AND HESITATION
AND ALL THAT HOLDS ME BACK.
SO MOTE IT BE!

Light the green candle next, and say:

O CANDLE OF GREEN
I GIVE THEE FLAME
FOR IN YOUR LIGHT THERE IS
HEALING, FERTILITY, AND PROSPERITY.
GRANT ME AMBITION AND GENEROSITY,
AND AS YOU BURN BRIGHT AND STRONG
MAY I BE BLESSED WITH
GOOD LUCK IN ABUNDANCE.
SO MOTE IT BE!

Finally, light the pink candle, and say:

O CANDLE OF PINK
I GIVE THEE FLAME
FOR IN YOUR LIGHT THERE IS
AFFECTION AND FRIENDSHIP,
HONOR AND UNSELFISHNESS.
AS YOU BURN BRIGHT AND STRONG
MAY MY SPIRIT AWAKEN
AND MAY MY HEART KNOW
THE TRUE MEANING OF LOVE
FOR LOVE IS THE TREASURE
AT THE END OF THE RAINBOW
AND ONLY LOVE CAN CONQUER ALL.
FOR LOVE IS LIGHT
AND LIGHT IS LOVE
AND LOVE SHALL BE THE LAW.
SO MOTE IT BE!

Visualize the magickal energy of each candle as a glowing aura of colored light surrounding its flame. Hold your arms out with palms up in a traditional Witches' prayer position and visualize a beam of colored light from each candle's aura flowing into your body through the tips of your fingers. (You may draw in the energy of each candle one at a time or all thirteen together if you wish.)

Continue the visualization until you feel your entire body is filled with warm, glowing multicolored light like a living rainbow of magickal energy.

When you feel that the time is right, slowly begin to withdraw from the visualization. It is now time to end the Rainbow Candle Spell and uncast the circle.

Take your athame and, starting in the direction of east, uncast the circle by tracing over it counterclockwise (also known as widdershins). As you do this say:

O SPIRITS OF THE AIR
WE LOVINGLY THANK THEE
FOR THY PRESENCE AND ENERGY
WE NOW BID THEE FAREWELL.
BLESSED BE!

O SPIRITS OF THE EARTH
WE LOVINGLY THANK THEE
FOR THY PRESENCE AND ENERGY.
WE NOW BID THEE FAREWELL.
BLESSED BE!

O SPIRITS OF THE WATER
WE LOVINGLY THANK THEE
FOR THY PRESENCE AND ENERGY.
WE NOW BID THEE FAREWELL.
BLESSED BE!

O SPIRITS OF THE FIRE
WE LOVINGLY THANK THEE
FOR THY PRESENCE AND ENERGY.

WE NOW BID THEE FAREWELL.
BLESSED BE!

IN PERFECT LOVE AND HARMING NONE
OUR SACRED SPELLWORK NOW IS DONE.
AS THE FUTURE BECOMES THE PRESENT,
AS THE PRESENT BECOMES THE PAST,
WE BID FAREWELL TO GODDESS AND GOD.
THIS CIRCLE OF MAGICK IS NOW UNCAST.
SO MOTE IT BE!

You may now extinguish the candles or allow them to burn out if you so desire.

(Photo by Gerina Dunwich)

Chapter 4

THE MAGICK
OF INCENSE

Incense is basically any combination of plant materials which are usually mixed together with essential oils and a base (such as pine sawdust, powdered quassia wood, or powdered sandalwood).

There are generally three forms of incense: the granular (also known as "raw") type which is sprinkled and burned on a small, glowing block of charcoal, the cone type, and the stick type. All three can be used in the practice of magick; however, the granular type is considered to be more traditional.

Of course, all Witches have their own personal preferences when it comes to which type of incense to use. I have worked with all three and found that I like cone incense the best for indoor rituals and spellwork, and stick incense for those performed outdoors.

Incense is an important part of the Craft and magickally powerful in any form; however, if you are planning on making your own homemade incense for spellwork (especially for the

Hans Baldung Grien, 1514

first time), the granular type is probably the easiest of the three above-mentioned types to make.

In Wiccan rituals and spellcastings, incense is often used to symbolize the ancient element of Air. It is burned as an offering to the Goddess and the Horned God (as well as to other Pagan deities), to invoke Sylphs (the elemental spirits of Air), and to create the proper mystical atmosphere for casting spells, divining, or invoking.

Incense can be used in just about any type of spell to enhance it, and when combined with visualization, the simple act of burning incense becomes a potent spell in itself.

Additionally, the breathing in of incense fumes is believed to help an individual achieve an altered state of consciousness (an old technique utilized by Witches and practitioners of ceremonial magick alike.)

Different incense fragrances each possess different magickal vibrations. There are also traditional Sabbat ritual incenses, and even corresponding incenses for each of the seven days of the week.

THE MAGICKAL PROPERTIES OF INCENSE

The following is a list of various incenses and their corresponding magickal properties.

ACACIA: Burned with sandalwood to stimulate the psychic powers.

AFRICAN VIOLET: Burned for protection and to promote spirituality within the home.

ALLSPICE: Burned to attract both good luck and money.

ALOES: Burned to attract good fortune, love, spiritual vibrations, and strength.

ALTHEA: Burned for protection and to stimulate the psychic powers.

ANISE SEEDS: Burned as a meditation incense.

BASIL: Burned to exorcise and protect against evil entities (such as demons and unfriendly ghosts), and to attract fidelity, love, good luck, sympathy, and wealth. This is also an excellent incense to use when performing love divinations.

BAY: Burned to facilitate the psychic powers, and to induce prophetic dream-visions.

BAYBERRY: Burned mainly to attract money.

BENZOIN: Burned for purification and to attract prosperity.

BISTORT: Burned (often with frankincense) as a powerful incense to aid divination.

BRACKEN: Burned in outdoor fires to magickally produce rain.

CEDAR: Burned for purification, to stimulate or strengthen the psychic powers, attract love, prevent nightmares, and heal various ailments, including head colds.

CINNAMON: Burned for protection and to attract money, stimulate or strengthen the psychic powers, and aid in healing.

CITRON: Burned in rituals to aid healing and also to strengthen the psychic powers.

CLOVE: Burned to dispel negativity, purify sacred and magickal spaces, attract money, and stop or prevent the spread of gossip.

COCONUT: Burned for protection.

COPAL: Burned for purification and to attract love.

DAMIANA: Burned to facilitate psychic visions.

DITTANY OF CRETE: Burned to conjure spirits and to aid in astral projection (especially when mixed with equal parts of benzoin, sandalwood, and vanilla).

DRAGON'S BLOOD: Burned to dispel negativity, exorcise evil supernatural entities, attract love, and restore male potency. Many Witches also burn dragon's blood for protection when spellcasting and invoking. When added to other incenses, dragon's blood makes their magickal powers all the stronger.

ELECAMPANE: Burned to strengthen the clairvoyant powers and scrying (divination by gazing) abilities.

FERN: Burned in outdoor fires to magickally produce rain. Also used to exorcise evil supernatural entities.

FRANKINCENSE: Burned to dispel negativity, purify magickal

spaces, protect against evil, aid meditation, induce psychic visions, attract good luck, and honor Pagan deities.

FUMITORY: Burned to exorcise demons, poltergeists, and evil supernatural entities.

GALANGAL: Burned to break the curses cast by sorcerers.

GINSENG ROOT: Burned to keep wicked spirits at bay, and for protection against all forms of evil.

GOTU KOLA: Burned to aid meditation.

HEATHER: Burned to conjure beneficial spirits, and to magickally produce rain.

HIBISCUS FLOWERS: Burned to attract love.

HOREHOUND: Burned as an offertory incense to the ancient Egyptian god Horus.

JASMINE: Burned to attract love and money, and also to induce dreams of a prophetic nature.

JUNIPER: Burned to stimulate or increase the psychic powers, and also to break curses and hexes cast by evil sorcerers.

LAVENDER: Burned to induce rest and sleep, and to attract love (especially of a man).

LILAC: Burned to stimulate or increase the psychic powers, and to attract harmony into one's life.

MACE: Burned to stimulate or increase the psychic powers.

MASTIC: Burned to conjure beneficial spirits, stimulate or increase the psychic powers, and intensify sexual desires. The magickal powers of other incenses are greatly increased when a bit of mastic is added.

MESQUITE: The magickal powers of all healing incenses are greatly increased when mesquite is added.

MINT: Burned to increase sexual desire, exorcise evil supernatural entities, conjure beneficial spirits, and attract money. Mint incense also possesses strong healing vibrations and protective powers.

MYRRH: Burned (often with frankincense) for purification, consecration, healing, exorcism, and banishing evil. Myrrh also aids meditation rituals, and was commonly burned on altars in ancient Egypt as an offering to the deities Isis and Ra.

NUTMEG: Burned to aid meditation, stimulate or increase the psychic powers, and attract prosperity.

PATCHOULI: Burned to attract money and love, and also to promote fertility.

PINE: Burned for purification, and to banish negative energies, exorcise evil supernatural entities, and attract money, as well as to break hexes and return them to their senders.

POPPY SEEDS: Burned to promote female fertility, and to attract love, good luck, and money.

ROSE: Burned to increase courage, induce prophetic dreams, and attract love. Rose incense is used in all forms of love enchantment and possesses the strongest love vibration of any magickal incense.

ROSEMARY: Burned to purify, aid in healing, prevent nightmares, preserve youthfulness, dispel depression, attract fairyfolk, and promote restful sleep and pleasant dreams.

RUE: Burned to help restore health.

SAGE: Burned for protection against all forms of evil, and to purify sacred spaces and ritual tools, promote wisdom, attract money, and aid in healing the body, mind, and soul.

SAGEBRUSH: Burned to aid healing, and to banish negative energies and evil supernatural entities.

SANDALWOOD: Burned to exorcise demons and evil ghosts, conjure beneficial spirits, and promote spiritual awareness. Sandalwood incense is also used by many Witches in healing rituals and in wish-magick.

SOLOMON'S SEAL: Burned mainly as an offertory incense to ancient Pagan deities.

STAR ANISE SEEDS: Burned to stimulate or increase the psychic powers.

STRAWBERRY: Burned to attract love.

SWEETGRASS: Burned to conjure beneficial spirits prior to spellcasting.

THYME: Burned for the purification of magickal spaces prior to rituals, to aid in healing, and to attract good health.

VANILLA: Burned to attract love, increase sexual desire, and improve the powers of the mind.

VERVAIN: Burned to exorcise evil supernatural entities.

VETIVERT: Burned to break curses, and for protection against sorcery (black magick) and thieves.

WILLOW: Burned to avert evil, attract love, and promote healing. It is also used by many Witches as an offertory incense for Pagan lunar deities.

WISTERIA: Burned for protection against all forms of evil.

WORMWOOD: Burned to stimulate or increase the psychic powers. When mixed with sandalwood and burned at night in a cemetery, wormwood is said to be able to conjure spirits from their graves.

TRADITIONAL SABBAT INCENSE

Each of the eight Witches' Sabbats that make up the Wheel of the Year have several traditional incenses. Many Witches burn them in brass or copper burners upon their altars as offerings to Pagan deities, and covens often pass a censor of the appropriate incense around the circle in order to remove negative energies from the magickal space (which is also known as "the temple") prior to the Sabbat rites.

Here are the eight Sabbats and the incenses which are used in each Sabbat rite:

CANDLEMAS: Angelica, basil, bay, benzoin, celandine, heather, myrrh, and all yellow flowers.

SPRING EQUINOX: Acorn, celandine, cinquefoil, crocus, daffodil, dogwood, Easter lily, honeysuckle, iris, jasmine, rose, strawberry, tansy, and violets.

BELTANE: Almond, angelica, ash tree, bluebells, cinquefoil, daisy, frankincense, hawthorn, ivy, lilac, marigold, meadowsweet, primrose, roses, satyrion root, woodruff, and yellow cowslips.

SUMMER SOLSTICE: Chamomile, cinquefoil, elder, fennel, hemp, larkspur, lavender, male fern, mugwort, pine, roses, Saint John's wort, wild thyme, wisteria, and verbena.

LAMMAS: Acacia flowers, aloes, cornstalks, cyclamen, fenugreek, frankincense, heather, hollyhock, myrtle, oak leaves, sunflower, and wheat.

AUTUMN EQUINOX: Acorns, asters, benzoin, ferns, honeysuckle, marigold, milkweed, mums, myrrh, oak leaves, passionflower, pine, roses, sage, Solomon's seal, and thistles.

SAMHAIN: Acorns, apples, broom, deadly nightshade, dittany, ferns, flax, fumitory, heather, mandrake, mullein, oak leaves, sage, and straw.

WINTER SOLSTICE: Bay, bayberry, blessed thistle, cedar, chamomile, evergreen, frankincense, holly, juniper, mistletoe, moss, oak, pine cones, rosemary, and sage.

DAILY INCENSE

SUNDAY: Lemon, frankincense.

MONDAY: African violet, honeysuckle, myrtle, willow, wormwood.

TUESDAY: Dragon's blood, patchouli.

WEDNESDAY: Jasmine, lavender, sweetpea.

THURSDAY: Cinnamon, musk, nutmeg, sage.

FRIDAY: Strawberry, sandalwood, rose, saffron, vanilla.

SATURDAY: Black poppy seeds, myrrh.

Chapter 5

DEDICATION
AND INITIATION

A Dedication is a sacred ceremony in which a Wiccan formally states his or her intent to follow the spiritual path of Wicca and to serve the Old Ones (the Goddess and the Horned God in any of their numerous aspects.)

Traditionally, a Dedication is performed under the light of a full moon; however, many Wiccans dedicate themselves during a Sabbat ritual, on their birthday, or as part of a formal initiation rite depending upon individual coven tradition.

If a Wiccan does not belong to a coven, he or she can perform what is known as a Rite of Self-Dedication. Most solitaries dedicate themselves in this way when they first enter into the Craft, and it should be known that Self-Dedication is no less meaningful or sacred than a formal one performed within the circle of a coven.

Ideally, you should write your own Dedication to be performed; however, if this is not possible, then it is acceptable to use one written by someone else, providing that you feel totally comfortable with that person's choice of words.

I perform the following ritual during every Summer Solstice Sabbat to rededicate myself to the Craft of Wicca. If you wish, you may also perform it as part of your own Dedication or Self-Dedication ceremony, or simply use it as a guideline for writing one of your own.

If you feel in your heart that something should be added, deleted, or changed in order to make it right for you, then by all means go ahead and do what you feel is needed.

SUMMER SOLSTICE DEDICATION RITE

Upon your altar, place a white candle, an incense burner filled with your favorite incense, a chalice of water (or wine), and a small container of salt (preferably sea salt).

Cast a circle around the altar using an athame or besom. Light the white candle, and say:

CAST NOW IS THIS MAGICK CIRCLE,
BRIGHT NOW IS THIS CANDLE OF WHITE.
THE ELEMENTS I NOW INVOKE
TO WATCH AND PROTECT THIS PAGAN RITE.

Light the incense in the burner. Holding it in your right hand, face East and invoke the elemental spirits of Air:

O MIGHTY ELEMENTAL SYLPHS:
GUARDIANS OF THE EAST
AND POWERS OF AIR AND MIND,
IN THE NAME OF THE OLD ONES
DO I CALL FORTH THY PRESENCE
AND THY MAGICK. BLESSED BE!

Return the incense burner to the altar. Now hold the white candle in your right hand and, facing South, invoke the elemental spirits of Fire:

> O MIGHTY ELEMENTAL SALAMANDERS:
> GUARDIANS OF THE SOUTH
> AND POWERS OF FIRE AND SPIRIT,
> IN THE NAME OF THE OLD ONES
> DO I CALL FORTH THY PRESENCE
> AND THY MAGICK. BLESSED BE!

Return the candle to the altar. Now hold the chalice of water (or wine) in your right hand and, facing West, invoke the elemental spirits of Water:

> O MIGHTY ELEMENTAL UNDINES:
> GUARDIANS OF THE WEST
> AND POWERS OF WATER AND SOUL,
> IN THE NAME OF THE OLD ONES
> DO I CALL FORTH THY PRESENCE
> AND THY MAGICK. BLESSED BE!

Drink a sip of the water (or wine) and return the chalice to the altar. Now hold the container of salt in your right hand, face North, and invoke the elemental spirits of Earth:

> O MIGHTY ELEMENTAL GNOMES:
> GUARDIANS OF THE NORTH
> AND POWERS OF EARTH AND BODY,
> IN THE NAME OF THE OLD ONES
> DO I CALL FORTH THY PRESENCE
> AND THY MAGICK. BLESSED BE!

Sprinkle a pinch of the salt at the North watchtower (directional point) of the magick circle and then return the container of salt to the altar.

Assuming a traditional Witch's prayer position (arms outstretched with palms up), recite the following words of dedication:

NOW AS SPRING CHANGES INTO SUMMER
AND THE GREAT SOLAR WHEEL
TURNS ONCE AGAIN,
AS NATURE'S SPELL OF GREEN
REJUVENATES OUR SPIRITS,
AND AS THE HOURS OF DARKNESS
GROW THEIR SHORTEST ON THIS
SACRED NIGHT OF THE YEAR
I DO INVOKE AND CALL UPON THEE
O GREAT GODDESS AND HORNED GOD.
IN THIS CONSECRATED CIRCLE
OF SHADOW AND FIRE
I DO PLEDGE MYSELF TO HONOR THEE,
TO LOVE THEE WITH ALL MY HEART,
AND TO SERVE THEE WELL
FOR AS LONG AS I SHALL LIVE.
I PROMISE TO RESPECT AND OBEY
THE LAW OF LOVE UNTO
ALL LIVING THINGS,
AND I SWEAR TO ABIDE
BY THE WICCAN REDE:
AN' IT HARM NONE,
DO WHAT THOU WILT.

If you are performing this rite outdoors, you may now take the chalice and pour the remaining water (or wine) onto the ground as a libation to the Goddess and the Horned God; otherwise, drink the remaining water (or wine) from the chalice and then return it to the altar.

In your own words, give thanks to each of the elemental spirits as you face the appropriate direction. Uncast the circle in a counterclockwise motion with the athame or besom, and say:

THIS CIRCLE IS NOW UNCAST.
THIS RITE IS NOW COMPLETE.
SO MOTE IT BE!

(Fortean Picture Library)

Initiation is one of the oldest and most sacred of Pagan rites; however, contrary to the popular historical beliefs associated with initiations into the Craft, modern-day Witches do not pay homage to or sign pacts with the Devil, renounce any faith (including Christianity), engage in obscene rituals, or perform blood sacrifices.

It is also highly doubtful that Witches ever did engage in such evil activities as propagandized by the Christian Church.

Many occult historians point out that the origins of such beliefs about Witchcraft initiation rites can be traced back to the infamous Witch-hunts of the Middle Ages and Renaissance.

During this period in history, countless persons accused of being in league with the Devil were forced to "confess" their diabolical practices under severe torture at the hands of sadistic inquisitors. After hours, and sometimes even days, of the most savage torture (which often consisted of such atrocities as the burning of genitals with red-hot irons, having fingernails torn out with a device known as a *turcas*, the boiling of fingers and hands in pots of bubbling oil, and the gouging out of eyeballs with irons) many women and men would eagerly confess to anything, no matter how bizarre it sounded, simply to bring an end to the excruciating pain being afflicted upon them.

Additionally, many of these tortured victims were delirious from pain and starvation or possibly even drugged with hallucinogenic elixirs at the time of their so-called confessions.

Records also prove that a number of persons accused of Witchcraft throughout Europe were elderly people of feeble mind and individuals who were mentally retarded or who suffered from mental illness of some form. The majority of these vulnerable persons were female.

In modern Wicca and Neo-Paganism, initiation marks both the beginning of an individual's journey into spiritual transformation and his or her official entry into a circle (coven).

A seventeenth-century woodcut depicting the artist's conception (or rather *mis*-conception) of a Witch's initiation rite. Here a young initiate pays homage to the Christian's Devil with a "kiss of shame"— a parody of the kissing of the Pope's foot. (R.P. Gauccius, *Compendium Maleficarum*, 1626)

Some circles perform only one initiation per member, while others (depending upon coven tradition) perform up to three degrees of advancement. In many (but not all) Wiccan covens, male Witches are initiated into the circle by the High Priestess, and female Witches are initiated into the circle by the High Priest.

The rite of initiation normally takes place after a Witch has gone through a period of apprenticeship during which he or she studies both the religious and magickal teachings of the Craft, learns the traditions of the coven, works on the development of inherent psychic abilities, and generally demonstrates to the elders of the circle his or her commitment to the

Wiccan path. Traditionally, a Witch's apprenticeship is carried out for a year and a day.

THE RITE OF INITIATION

Like the previous Rite of Dedication, the Rite of Initiation can easily be adapted to suit any Wiccan tradition.

Before the rite begins, the following items should be placed upon the altar: a black cast-iron cauldron, an incense burner filled with frankincense and myrrh incense, a white votive candle for each person being initiated into the circle (with their names inscribed in runes upon the wax), a chalice filled with water, a small bowl filled with salt, an altar bell, and two altar candles (a silver one to represent the Goddess and a gold one to represent the Horned God).

The High Priest lights the two altar candles as the High Priestess casts the magick circle with an athame. The High Priest then rings the altar bell three times and the High Priestess invokes the four elemental spirits in the same manner outlined in the Rite of Dedication.

All members of the coven should form a human circle with all hands joined together. In the center of this circle should be the High Priestess, the High Priest, the initiate, and the altar. The initiate kneels before the High Priestess, who asks:

IN THE PRESENCE OF THE GODDESS WHO
BLESSES US WITH BIRTH, DEATH, AND
REBIRTH: IN THE PRESENCE OF HER
CONSORT, THE HORNED GOD: AND IN THE
PRESENCE OF THE FOUR ELEMENTALS, THE
MIGHTY DEAD ONES, AND THY BROTHERS
AND SISTERS OF THE CRAFT, ART THOU

READY WITH PERFECT LOVE AND PERFECT
TRUST TO TAKE THY VOWS AND EMBARK ON
A JOURNEY INTO SELF AND TOWARD THE
DIVINE FORCE?

The initiate replies affirmatively, and the High Priestess says:

THEN SO BE IT.

The initiate then recites aloud the following vows and oath
of secrecy which he or she has written down on parchment,
using dragon's blood ink:

AS THE GODDESS AND HER CONSORT
ARE MY WITNESSES,
I DO SOLEMNLY SWEAR THAT I,
BEING OF SOUND MIND AND FREE WILL,
DESIRE WITH THE UTMOST SINCERITY
TO BE INITIATED INTO THE SACRED
CIRCLE KNOWN AS (*name of coven*).
I PLEDGE TO SERVE THE GODDESS
AND HER CONSORT, THE HORNED GOD.
I PROMISE TO NEVER STRAY FROM
THE WICCAN REDE WHICH STATES:
AN' IT HARM NONE, LOVE,
AND DO WHAT THOU WILT.
I WILL WORK ONLY WITH POSITIVE
ENERGIES AND WHITE MAGICK,
AND I WILL STRIVE TO USE
THE POWERS OF WITCHCRAFT
FOR THE GOOD OF OTHERS.
FOR THE BENEFIT AND SAFETY
OF THIS CIRCLE AND ALL WHO

ARE A PART OF IT
DO I HEREBY SWEAR
THE FOLLOWING OATH OF SECRECY:
I WILL AT ALL TIMES KEEP SECRET
THE LOCATION AND DESCRIPTION
OF THIS COVENSTEAD.
I WILL GUARD THE SECRETS OF
THE CRAFT AND THIS CIRCLE,
AND I WILL NEVER, AT ANY TIME,
REVEAL TO AN OUTSIDER THE TRUE
IDENTITY OF ANY WOMAN OR MAN
WHO GATHERS WITHIN THIS SACRED
SPACE UNLESS I AM GIVEN
PERMISSION TO DO SO
BY THAT INDIVIDUAL.
I FURTHER SWEAR THAT SHOULD I,
FOR ANY REASON, AT ANY TIME,
LEAVE THIS CIRCLE OR THE PAGAN PATH,
I WILL CONTINUE TO HONOR THIS OATH
FOR AS LONG AS I SHALL LIVE.

The High Priestess now says to the initiate:

SEAL YOUR OATH WITH A KISS
AND RISE NOW TO YOUR FEET.

The initiate should place a kiss from his or her lips on the parchment and then stand facing the High Priestess who pours about one-fourth cup of alcohol into the cauldron, lights it with a match, and says:

YOU MAY NOW PLACE THY WRITTEN OATH
INTO THE CAULDRON OF TRANSFORMATION

SO THAT IT MAY BE CONSUMED BY FIRE
AND DELIVERED TO OUR GODDESS
AND HER CONSORT.

The initiate should crumple up the parchment and then drop it into the flaming cauldron. (The alcohol fire should burn for approximately three minutes before dying out on its own. If, for some reason, the fire should need to be extinguished before then, simply place a lid over the cauldron or sprinkle some sand on the fire.)

The High Priest takes the athame from the altar and hands it to the High Priestess. She then uses it to draw a pentagram in the air in front of the initiate, and says:

BY THE SACRED POWER
OF BLADE AND PENTACLE
DO I BLESS AND EMPOWER THEE.

The High Priestess hands the athame back to the High Priest who returns it to its place on the altar. He now lights the incense in the burner and hands it to the High Priestess. She then uses it to draw a pentagram in the air in front of the initiate, and says:

BY THE ANCIENT ELEMENT OF AIR
AND THE GUARDIANS OF THE EAST
I DO BLESS AND EMPOWER THEE.

The High Priestess hands the incense burner back to the High Priest. He returns it to its place on the altar, lights the votive candle, and hands it to the High Priestess. She then uses it to draw a pentagram in the air in front of the initiate, and says:

BY THE ANCIENT ELEMENT OF FIRE
AND THE GUARDIANS OF THE SOUTH
I DO BLESS AND EMPOWER THEE.

The High Priestess hands the candle back to the High Priest. He returns it to its place on the altar and then hands the chalice of water to the High Priestess who uses it to draw a pentagram in the air in front of the initiate. Holding the chalice in her right hand, the High Priestess dips the fingertips of her left hand into the water and then sprinkles a bit of it over the initiate, and says:

BY THE ANCIENT ELEMENT OF WATER
AND THE GUARDIANS OF THE WEST
I DO BLESS AND EMPOWER THEE.

The High Priestess hands the chalice back to the High Priest. He returns it to its place on the altar and then hands the bowl of salt to the High Priestess. She uses it to draw a pentagram in the air in front of the initiate. She then takes a pinch of the salt between her fingers and sprinkles it over the initiate, and says:

BY THE ANCIENT ELEMENT OF EARTH
AND THE GUARDIANS OF THE NORTH
I DO BLESS AND EMPOWER THEE.

The High Priestess hands the bowl of salt back to the High Priest who returns it to its place on the altar. The High Priestess now says to the initiate:

AS HIGH PRIESTESS OF THIS COVEN
I OFFICIALLY RECOGNIZE THEE A WITCH

AND I DO HEREBY WELCOME THEE
WITH OPEN ARMS AND LOVING HEART
INTO THIS CIRCLE AS ONE OF US.
SO MOTE IT BE!

The High Priestess embraces the newly-initiated member of the coven. The High Priest embraces him or her next, and then each member of the coven, clockwise around the circle, takes a turn giving the new member an embrace and welcoming him or her to the circle.

The four elemental spirits are thanked and bade farewell by the High Priestess (in the same manner outlined in the Rite of Dedication) and the circle is then uncast counterclockwise with the athame.

Chapter 6

A CALENDAR OF THE MAGICKAL YEAR

In this chapter you will find ritual outlines for all eight of the Sabbats, as well as spells and magickal rites to be performed at other times throughout the year. On the days that fall in between, you are encouraged to work your own personal magick (such as healings and divinations as needed), different lunar and astrological rituals as the moon changes signs (see chapter 1: Lunar Spellwork), birthday blessings for loved ones, weather-working magick (as needed), Wiccanings (sacred rituals for naming and blessing a Witch's newborn child), handfastings, empowerments, and so forth.

NEW YEAR'S RESOLUTION SPELL

January 1

On the first day of the new year many Wiccans from all over

the world like to perform a ritual to bless the coming year with peace, love, health, and prosperity for all.

As this is also the traditional time for ending bad habits and beginning good ones, a spell to ensure that you keep all of your New Year's resolutions would be appropriate.

On the morning of January 1, take a new white candle and hold it between your hands as you concentrate on whatever resolutions you have made to yourself the night before. (If you wish, you may also write or engrave your resolutions on the side of the candle. For engraving, I recommend using the sharp end of a nut pick; however, you can use any tool that works best for you, including the tip of your ritual knife's blade, as long as you take care not to cut your fingers or hands.)

When you feel that the candle has absorbed your personal energies, place it on the center of your altar. Anoint it with a few drops of rosemary oil, and then light it. As its flame burns bright, recite the following magickal prayer over the candle:

AS THIS NEW CANDLE BURNS ON THIS NEW DAY OF THE NEW YEAR, I, *state your name*, DO HEREBY MAKE THE FOLLOWING RESOLUTION/S: *state your resolution/s*.

AS THE GODDESS AND THE HORNED GOD ARE MY WITNESSES, I MAKE THE FOLLOWING PROMISE TO NO ONE OTHER THAN MYSELF—I SWEAR THAT THE RESOLUTION/S I HAVE MADE WILL NOT BE BROKEN. I HAVE A DUTY TO MYSELF AND TO THOSE WHO LOVE ME TO KEEP MY WILLPOWER STRONG AND TO STAY FOCUSED ON MY GOAL. THE POWER IS WITHIN ME.

IF I SHOULD EVER FEEL MYSELF WEAKENING, I AM CONFIDENT THAT I CAN CALL UPON THE POWERS OF THE GODDESS AND THE HORNED GOD TO STRENGTHEN ME.

AS THE ANCIENT GOD JANUS LOOKS BOTH TO THE PAST AND
TO THE FUTURE, I TOO SHALL LOOK TO THE PAST TO LEARN
AND GROW FROM MY MISTAKES AND FAILURES, AND LOOK TO
THE FUTURE WITH THIS KNOWLEDGE TO GUIDE ME AND THE
POWER TO CREATE POSITIVE TRANSFORMATION IN MY LIFE.
THE FUTURE BEGINS NOW.

SO MOTE IT BE!

Allow the candle to burn itself completely down. If you
must extinguish its flame for any reason before it burns out on
its own, do so by using a candle snuffer or by pinching out the
flame with your moistened fingertips.

Blowing out the flame of a magickally-energized candle is
regarded as an insult to the gods and a symbolic act of blowing your magick away, which, of course, is not what one strives
for when casting spells.

Light the candle once again as soon as you are able to,
repeat the prayer, and then allow the candle to burn down the
rest of the way.

DAY OF THE TRIPLE GODDESS

January 6

The Day of the Triple Goddess is observed by many Wiccans
and Neo-Pagans of various traditions each year on this date.
This is a time to pay homage to the Goddess in Her three
aspects which consist of the Maiden or Virgin (represented by
the new and waxing moon), the Mother (represented by the
full moon), and the Crone (represented by the waning and
dark of the moon).

The Goddess is recognized around the world in many trinities, such as the Morrigan of Ireland who is personified by Ana (the Virgin), Babd (the Mother), and Macha (the Crone); and the ancient Greek lunar trinity of Artemis/Selene/Hecate, just to give two examples.

The following Triple Goddess Ritual can easily be adapted to suit whichever Goddess trinity you feel most drawn to.

Place three candles (one white, one green, and one black) upon your altar. Light the white one first in honor of the Goddess in Her Maiden aspect, and say:

I LIGHT THIS CANDLE FOR THE MAIDEN:
A GODDESS OF BEGINNINGS
AND THE BIRTH OF SPRING.
SHE IS FERTILITY, SHE IS GROWTH.
SHE REFLECTS THE MYSTICAL BEAUTY
OF THE SACRED WOMAN-SPIRIT.

Next, light the green candle in honor of the Goddess in Her Mother aspect, and say:

I LIGHT THIS CANDLE FOR THE MOTHER:
SHE IS NURTURING AND PROTECTING.
SHE IS THE GIVER OF LIFE, THE DIVINE
MATRIX OF NEVERENDING MYSTERY.
WITH HER LIGHT OF WHITE SHE HEALS.
HER BREASTS FLOW WITH THE MILK
OF SUMMER'S SWEETNESS.

Finally, light the black candle in honor of the Goddess in Her Crone aspect, and say:

I LIGHT THIS CANDLE FOR THE CRONE:
WITH WISDOM SHE RULES

LIKE AN ANCIENT QUEEN.
INTO WINTER'S DARKNESS
SHE GUIDES US
WHEN OUR AUTUMNS
IN THIS WORLD END.

SO MOTE IT BE!

SAINT AGNES' EVE

January 20

Saint Agnes was a Roman Catholic child martyr who was beheaded in the year 304 A.D. for refusing to marry.

The eve of her feast day is an ideal (and traditional) time for Witches to perform all forms of romantic enchantments, especially love divination. According to a very old legend, it is on this night of the year when an unmarried woman is able to catch a glimpse of her husband-to-be in a dream.

To perform such a divination, light a pink candle before you go to bed. If you wish, you may anoint the candle with any herbal oil associated with the art of love magick, such as orris, sandalwood, vetivert, or ylang-ylang. Hold a hand mirror up to your face. Gaze into the mirror and recite the following incantation:

DEAR SAINT AGNES, SWEET AND FAIR
I CALL TO THEE WITH HUMBLE PRAYER:
WITH CLARITY I WISH TO SEE
THE FACE OF MY TRUE LOVE TO BE.
TONIGHT LET HIM BE DREAM-REVEALED;
WITH A KISS THIS RHYME IS SEALED.
SO MOTE IT BE!

Place a kiss upon the mirror's glass and then place the mirror with the glass side up, underneath your pillow. In your own words give thanks to Saint Agnes for listening to your prayer, and then go to sleep with an open mind.

If there is a marriage in your future (anytime within the next twelve months), you should receive a vivid dream about the man who is destined to become your partner in matrimony.

CANDLEMAS CANDLE SPELL

February 2

Candlemas is a Sabbat which celebrates the coming of Springtime, and represents new beginnings and spiritual growth. Additionally, it is an ideal time for those who follow the path of Wicca to perform a personal power raising ritual such as the one outlined below:

After casting a circle, take a new white candle and write or etch your name upon it. You may use your given name and/or your Craft name, if you have taken one. If you desire, you may also add your personal astrological symbols, rune designs, and so forth.

Anoint the candle with a few drops of your favorite candle anointing oil, and then place it on the center of your altar. Light its wick, and as it burns, visualize all of your goals being achieved and recite the following incantation:

WITH FIRE AND WAX THIS SPELL BEGINS
TO SUMMON THE MAGICK FROM DEEP WITHIN.
WITH CANDLE OF NAMES ON WITCHES' ALTAR
MY POWER IS STRONG, I WILL NOT FALTER.

AS THIS CANDLE FLAME LIGHTS THE DARKNESS
SO SHALL MY DREAMS SEE
THE LIGHT OF REALIZATION
AND RADIATE WITH POWER!

AS THIS CANDLE WAX MELTS AWAY
SO SHALL MY OBSTACLES MELT AWAY
AND ALL THAT HOLDS ME BACK
FROM ACHIEVING MY GOALS AND
ATTAINING THAT WHICH I DESIRE!

SO MOTE IT BE!

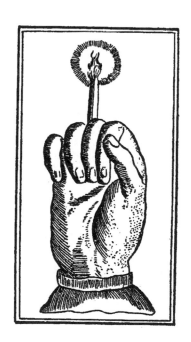

A VALENTINE SPELL FOR LOVERS

February 14

To help attract a passionate lover into your life, perform this spell at midnight on Saint Valentine's Day, preferably outdoors in a quiet location where you will not be disturbed.

Take a blank Valentine card (either store-bought or homemade, and the fancier the better) and draw a pentagram inside it using dragon's blood (a magickal ink traditionally used by Witches in all forms of love enchantment, and available at most occult shops.) As you do this, focus all of your thoughts upon the type of lover you wish to attract, such as his or her physical attributes, personality traits, and so forth. But take care not to name or visualize any specific individual.

In each of the pentagram's five points, draw a smaller pentagram, and then in its center, write your name five times.

Sprinkle some dried thyme (an herb associated with love spells) inside the card as you say:

WITH WORDS OF RHYME
AND HERBS OF THYME
TO CONJURE PASSION
THIS SPELL I FASHION.

Close the card and place it inside an envelope. Light a red candle (strawberry or apple-scented works the best) and then drip some of the melted wax onto the envelope to form the symbol of a heart.

Using the flame of the same candle, set the envelope and card on fire. Place them in a fireproof container and as they burn, recite the following incantation:

AS THE FIRE OF DESIRE
BURNS THIS HERB-FILLED VALENTINE
MAY THE POWER OF ITS MAGICK
BRING A LOVING ONE SO FINE.
SO MOTE IT BE!

After the flames have died out and the ashes have cooled, gather them up and then sprinkle them outside of your house at each of the four directional points, starting with East, and then South, West, and finally North.

PENTAGRAM NIGHT

February 26

As a symbolic gesture to reaffirm your dedication to the craft of Wicca and the Old Ones, dip the fingertip of your right index finger into a small cauldron pot (or other container) filled with ashes from a Yule log.

If Yule-log ashes are unavailable, you may substitute ashes from a fireplace in which magickal herbs, a Wiccan Dedication on parchment, or something used in a spell of positive magick was burned.

Use the ashes to draw the sacred symbol of the Witches' Pentagram (five-pointed star within a circle) over your heart at the first stroke of midnight. As you do this, repeat thrice the following incantation:

AS NOW BEGINS THE WITCHING HOUR
A CIRCLE AND STAR OF ANCIENT POWER
OVER MY HEART I DRAW WITH PRIDE:
TO THE LIGHT OF WHITE
MAY MY SOUL IT GUIDE.
SO MOTE IT BE!

SALEM MEMORIAL RITE

March 1

From the fifteenth to the seventeenth century it is estimated that over nine million people worldwide (most of them young females) were put to their deaths after being tried and found guilty of the "unspeakable crime of Witchcraft." Nearly all were subjected to the cruelest and most unthinkable acts of torture, and the small percentage of individuals who were judged not guilty usually died proving their innocence. Throughout Europe, the two most popular methods of executing Witches were burning them alive at the stake and beheading.

On the first day of March in the year 1692, the infamous Salem Witch hunt and trials officially began. By the time the "God-fearing" (but bloodthirsty, nonetheless) Puritans who were behind it finally came to their senses and ended their sadistic torturing and execution of innocent people, nineteen women had been hanged on Salem's Gallows Hill and one man who would not give testimony had been crushed to death underneath a pile of heavy stones that had been placed, one by one, on top of him until every bone in his body fractured and his eyeballs popped out of their sockets.

Each year on the anniversary date that marks the beginning of the Salem Witch trials, many modern day Witches, Wiccans and Neo-Pagans alike feel a need within their hearts to do something special in memory of the tragic event, such as offering prayers of healing to the spirits of the victims and to all of their descendants as well.

The following is my own personal ritual that I perform each year on this date: After the sun disappears beyond the horizon and the darkness of night veils the sky, I light some

In the small New England village of Salem in 1692, the infamous Witch trials claimed the lives of nineteen women and one man. Those who were "lucky" enough to escape the hands of death were brutally tortured and often raped in jail just the same. Upon release, many discovered that everything they owned had been permanently confiscated and used as payment for the services rendered by their jailers and torturers.

incense on my altar along with a new white candle that has been anointed with a few drops of clove, myrrh, or sandal-wood oil.

After a period of meditation, I begin visualizing a white light of healing power forming a circle around me. I "breathe in" some of the light through the palm of my left hand, and then I "exhale" it through the palm of my right hand, directing it by the power of my will toward the restless spirits of all Witch trial victims and their families. As I do this I recite the following Witches' prayer of rhyme:

WITCHES OF SALEM, INNOCENT ALL,
MURDERED IN THE NAME OF THE LORD.
CENTURIES LATER WE HEAR YOUR CALL:
THE TRUTH REVEALED IS YOUR REWARD.
BE FROM YOUR CHAINS OF PAIN RELEASED,
MAY ALL YOUR SPIRITS NOW FIND PEACE.
AND FROM THE PAST LET THERE BE LEARNING,
WE CRY: NEVER AGAIN THE BURNING!
SO MOTE IT BE!

SEED BLESSING RITUAL

Spring Equinox

The Spring Equinox (also known as the Vernal Equinox) is a traditional time for many Witches to perform special blessings over the seeds which they gathered in the fall of the previous year. (Store-bought packets of seeds may be blessed as well.)

Perform the following blessing at sunset in the center of a clockwise-cast circle: Place the seeds to be blessed in a basket or cauldron. If the seeds are contained within a packet, you may place the entire packet of seeds into the basket or cauldron. Using an athame or wand, draw thrice a pentagram in the air over the seeds, and say:

AS WINTER'S REIGN COMES TO AN END
AND SPRING BRINGS WARMTH AND LIGHT,
THE SPIRITS OF THESE SEEDS I DO CALL FORTH
ON OSTARA'S SACRED NIGHT.
FROM YOUR REST SO DARK AND LONG
AWAKEN NOW WITH BIRTH!
YOU SHALL, IN TIME, GROW GREEN AND STRONG
IN THE SOIL OF MOTHER EARTH.
SO MOTE IT BE!

MOONRISE PRAYER

March 31

Each year on the thirty-first of March, the people of ancient Rome would honor the beautiful and powerful goddess of the moon and lunar magick with a sacred ceremony known as the Feast of Luna.

The following ritual is designed for all modern Witches who desire to pay homage to the Moon Goddesses who guide, protect, and teach us in various mystical ways:

At the first stroke of midnight, light a brand new silver candle (to represent the moon) and, either standing outdoors under the moon (preferably) or indoors at a window facing the moon, hold the burning candle up in salute to Her and then recite the following honoring rhyme:

RAYS OF MOONLIGHT
SILVERY-WHITE
EMBLAZON THE NIGHT
WITH MAGICK BRIGHT.

LADY LUNA WAXES AND WANES;
OUR GOALS SHE HELPS US TO ATTAIN.
HUNTRESS DIANA FILLS US WITH MIGHT;
ARTEMIS GLORIOUSLY GOVERNS THE NIGHT.

MOTHER SELENE DANCES ABOVE;
SHE BLESSES HER CHILDREN
WITH LUNAR LOVE.
SACRED PARVATI REIGNS SUPREME;
ANCIENT LUCINA GIVES BIRTH
TO OUR DREAMS.

DARK CRONE HECATE PROTECTS US ALL;
DESTROYER, RESTORER,

SHE HEEDS OUR CALL.
ARADIA TEACHES US WITCHY WAYS;
OUR KNOWLEDGE INCREASES
WITH EVERY PHASE.

HAIL TO THE MOON
AND HER MYSTICAL POWER.
I OFFER THIS TUNE
AT THE WITCHING HOUR.

SO MOTE IT BE!

EARTH DAY BLESSING

April 22

Earth Day (which is designed to increase community awareness of important environmental issues) is dedicated to Mother Earth and an appropriate time for Wiccans throughout the world to perform Gaia-healing rituals, such as the one outlined below:

Draw a pentagram symbol (five-pointed star) on the ground using your athame, ritual sword, or wand. Draw a circle (clockwise) around the pentagram and then place a new white candle in the center of the star.

Sit before the candle on the ground with your legs crossed "Indian style" or in the yoga lotus position. Light the candle, and as you gaze into its flame, focus your thoughts and energies upon the Earth, her rugged beauty and natural wonders.

Cupping your hands together, take up some soil and recite the following magickal verses of blessing:

BLESS THE EARTH
BLESS THE EARTH
SHE IS OUR MOTHER
FERTILE AND GREEN.

BLESS THE EARTH
BLESS THE EARTH
SHE IS OUR HEALER
SHE IS OUR QUEEN.

DANCING, DANCING
DAY AND NIGHT
ALONG HER MAGICK CIRCLE BRIGHT,
GIVING BIRTH TO LAND AND SEA,
MOTHER EARTH, I HONOR THEE.

BLESS THE EARTH
BLESS THE EARTH
SHE IS OUR TEACHER
ANCIENT AND WISE.
SHE MUST BE CHERISHED;
LET HER NOT PERISH:
SHE IS OUR GODDESS
IN DISGUISE.

SO MOTE IT BE!

BELTANE FIRE MAGICK

Beltane, one of the four major Sabbats observed each year by Wiccans throughout the world, celebrates the sacred union of the Goddess and the Horned God, and is derived from a Druid fire festival from long ago which was carried out in the belief of promoting fertility.

The lighting of bonfires is an old Beltane tradition, as is dancing clockwise around a brightly-decorated Maypole (an obvious phallic fertility symbol).

On the first day of May (or anytime after sunset on Beltane Eve, April 30) write your secret wishes, blessings, thanksgivings, prayers for healings, and so forth upon small slips of

(Photo by Gerina Dunwich)

green paper or leaves. Roll them into little "scrolls" and tuck them into a wreath fashioned from braided vines or twigs. Cast the wreath into a blazing Beltane fire, and say:

SACRED FIRE, BLAZING SO BRIGHT
ACCEPT THIS OFFERING TO YOUR LIGHT.
BURN INTO ASH,
TURN INTO SMOKE,
O BELTANE FIRE-DRAKES I INVOKE.

CERRIDWEN'S CAULDRON RITUAL

June 20

Each year on the twentieth of June, many Witches and Pagans (especially in Ireland and Great Britain) celebrate what is known as The Day of Cerridwen. It is a time for paying homage to the ancient Celtic goddess of fertility.

An old illustration of a young Witch assisted by her familiars as she brews a cauldron of enchantments.

Place a green candle on your altar along with a small cauldron or fireproof incense burner filled with dried vervain (this is the herb most sacred to Cerridwen). Light the candle and burn the vervain as you say:

TO GODDESS CERRIDWEN I DO PRAY
GUIDE ME THROUGH ANOTHER DAY,
LET ALL EVIL TURN AWAY
AND KEEP MISFORTUNE WELL AT BAY.
LET MY HEART BE BLESSED WITH HEALTH
AND LET MY PURSE BE BLESSED WITH WEALTH.
WITH WORDS OF RHYME I PRAY TO THEE
THOU ART SUBLIME, SO MOTE IT BE!

OCEAN PRAYER

Summer Solstice

Perform this spell on a beach, either at night or during daylight hours:

Draw a large circle in the sand, using an athame, ritual sword, wand, or even your finger. Sit down within the circle facing the ocean. Focus your mind upon its power and beauty, and recite the following Wiccan prayer. (When finished, you may honor the Ocean Goddess with a handful of flower petals or tiny seashells tossed into the water as a love offering.)

OCEAN GODDESS, WET AND WILD,
I AM YOUR HUMBLE HUMAN CHILD.
ENCHANTRESS OF THE CORAL LAIR
I HONOR THEE WITH PAGAN PRAYER.

I KNEEL BEFORE THEE ON THE SHORE
BENEATH THE SEAGULLS AS THEY SOAR

ACROSS THE HEAVENS HIGH ABOVE
TO PARTAKE OF YOUR MYSTICAL LOVE.

OCEAN GODDESS, GIVER OF LIFE,
WATER'S DAUGHTER, MOTHER, AND WIFE
ROMANCING IN THE UNDERSEA CAVES
AND DANCING IN THE SALTY WAVES.

YOU BLESS MY SOUL WITH OCEAN-PEACE
AS YOUR MOON-TIDES EBB AND INCREASE.
O GODDESS OF THE SEA SUPREME,
YOUR WATERS QUENCH THE THIRST
OF MY DREAMS.

SO MOTE IT BE!

ST. JOHN'S EVE

June 23

The eve of Saint John's Day (or Midsummer's Day) is a traditional time for Witches in all parts of the world to gather herbs from their gardens or from the wild to use in potions, dream pillows, poppets, and other forms of spellcraft.

According to ancient legend, the magickal and mystical properties of all plants are greatest on this particular night of the year.

AN HERB-GATHERING SPELL   To be recited on Saint John's Eve, thrice before and thrice after gathering your herbs for magickal workings:

HERBS OF MAGICK, HERBS OF POWER,
ROOT AND BARK, LEAF AND FLOWER,
WORK FOR ME WHEN CHARMS ARE SPOKEN,
POTIONS BREWED AND CURSES BROKEN!

INDEPENDENCE DAY RITUAL

July 4

Drape an American flag over your altar and upon it place three candles: one red, one white, and one blue. Together they symbolize the United States of America, her people, and Lady Liberty as a goddess of freedom.

Before beginning the ritual, light some incense and meditate before the altar for awhile. Focus your mind upon the positive things about your country, as well as the many problems that are facing her today. Try to think of ways to improve matters. Visualize all negativity completely eliminated, and all men, women, and children, not only in the United States, but throughout the entire world as well, living their lives happy, healthy, and free.

When you feel you are ready to begin the ritual, light the red candle and then say out loud:

> I LIGHT THIS CANDLE WITH A PRAYER
> FOR LOVE TO UNITE ALL INDIVIDUALS
> OF THIS GREAT NATION AND OF THE WORLD
> REGARDLESS OF THEIR RACE, CULTURE,
> SPIRITUAL PATH, OR SEXUAL PREFERENCE.
> LADY LIBERTY, GODDESS
> AND SYMBOL OF FREEDOM,
> I ASK THEE TO GUIDE US.
> LET US BE BRAVE AND STRONG.
> LET US FOREVER REMAIN
> THE LAND OF THE FREE.

Light the white candle next, and say:

> I LIGHT THIS CANDLE WITH A PRAYER
> TO HELP HEAL THIS COUNTRY FROM THE

WOUNDS OF WAR, POVERTY, POLLUTION,
CRIME, BIGOTRY, DISEASE,
AND ALL THINGS NEGATIVE.
LET THE HEALING NOW BEGIN.
LET OUR SPIRITUAL STRENGTH BE GREAT.
LET US GROW IN WISDOM
AND CONTINUE TO SEEK TRUTH
AND JUSTICE FOR ALL.

Finally, light the blue candle, and say:

I LIGHT THIS CANDLE WITH A PRAYER
FOR PEACE BETWEEN ALL NATIONS
AND ALL CHILDREN OF THE GREAT MOTHER
WE CALL OUR PLANET EARTH.
LET US BEGIN TO LIVE TOGETHER
IN HARMONY AS BROTHERS AND SISTERS
WITH LOVE, UNDERSTANDING, AND
RESPECT FOR EACH OTHER.
LET US BE ABLE TO LEARN FROM THE PAST
AND BE ABLE TO LOOK TO THE FUTURE
WITH OPEN HEARTS AND OPEN MINDS.
LET US BE UNITED AS ONE NATION
UNDER GODDESS AND GOD.

SO MOTE IT BE!

LAMMAS CORN DOLLY

August 1

On this Sabbat (which marks the beginning of the season of harvest and pays homage to the fertility aspect of the sacred union between the Goddess and the Horned God) it is a tradition among many Wiccans to make what is known as a "corn dolly" (a small human-shaped figure fashioned from braided straw or the last sheaf of corn from a harvest). For good luck in the coming twelve months, the corn dolly from the past year's Lammas Sabbat is usually burned as an offering to the spirit of the corn or to the Mother Goddess of the harvest.

To make a traditional Witch's corn dolly, bind together into a sheaf the last cornstalk reaped. Plait it into a female figure to represent the spirit of the corn, and then lay it on the center of your altar.

Place an orange candle to its left and a yellow candle to its right. Light the candles, cast a clockwise circle around the altar to establish a sacred temple, and then invoke the four elements:

I NOW CALL FORTH
THE SACRED SPIRITS
OF THE ANCIENT AND
MYSTICAL ELEMENTS
OF AIR, FIRE, WATER,
AND EARTH.

Light some rose or sandalwood incense (the traditional incenses of the Lammas Sabbat) and, holding the corn dolly in both of your hands, pass it three times through the fragrant smoke, and then say:

O GREAT MOTHER, SPIRIT OF THE CORN
INTO THIS DOLLY YE SHALL BE REBORN.
FOR GOOD HARVEST, NOW TO THEE
MAY WE GIVE THANKS. SO MOTE IT BE!

You may now perform an additional Lammas rite if you so desire, or you may simply give thanks to the elementals, dismiss them, and then uncast the circle.

After Lammas is over, wrap the corn dolly in an orange-colored cloth and then place it inside a basket or a special box. Put it in a dark and undisturbed place (such as an attic or an old, unused barn) and save it until the following Lammas.

If you make a new corn dolly each harvest season, you may burn the old one as part of your Lammas Sabbat rite.

NEW MOON WISHING SPELL

August

According to an ancient superstition, if a person makes a secret wish while gazing up at the new moon in August, his or her wish will come true before the end of the year.

On the first night of the new moon, light a white candle. As its flame burns, gaze deeply into it and focus all of your thoughts and feelings upon whatever it is that you are strongly wishing to have, to do, or to make happen. Take care, however, not to wish for anything that would directly or indirectly bring harm to, or interfere with the free will of, any individual.

Raise your arms up to the sky with both of your palms facing up, and say:

GODDESS OF THE NEW MOON FAIR
I ASK THEE HARKEN TO THIS PRAYER.
MAY THAT WHICH I DESIRE BE GRANTED,
WITH INTENT THESE WORDS ARE CHANTED.

Now state your wish three times, and then say:

THRICE MY RHYMING SPELL IS SPUN
TO MAKE THIS WISH COME TRUE FOR ME.
THANKS I GIVE FOR IT IS DONE.
THIS IS MY WILL. SO MOTE IT BE!

HARVEST MOON RITUAL

The full moon which occurs during the month of September is known as the Harvest Moon. Since olden times it has been believed to be the source of the greatest magickal power.

Many Wiccans and Pagans from around the world perform a Harvest Moon ritual of one kind or another on this night. Often it is for empowerment, protection, and/or personal guidance.

The following ritual is one that I designed for my coven Mandragora. If you are a solitary practitioner of the Craft, you can easily adapt this ritual to your own use by changing the words "we" to "I," "our" to "my," and "us" to "me."

Cast a clockwise circle and, in the center, light a silver or white candle to represent the Harvest Moon. With the palms of your hands turned up, raise your arms high to the sky and call upon the Moon Goddess:

ARTEMIS, DIANA, LUNA, LUCINA,
BY MANY NAMES YOU HAVE BEEN KNOWN.
O MOTHER ASPECT OF THE TRIPLE GODDESS
THIS HUMBLE PRAYER I OFFER TO THEE.

Visualize your circle surrounded by protective Goddess energy in the form of a white light which will prevent negative energies from entering into the circle. The white light also serves to keep your positive energies within the circle. As you do this, say:

I ASK THAT OUR CIRCLE BE BLESSED
WITH YOUR SACRED LIGHT
SO THAT WE MAY ALWAYS BE UNITED BY LOVE
AND PROTECTED FROM THE DARKNESS OF NEGATIVITY
AND ALL THINGS OF AN EVIL NATURE.

AS YOU SHINE ABOVE, BRIGHT AND FULL,
SO MAY OUR HEARTS, OUR MINDS,
OUR BODIES, AND OUR SPIRITS
BE BRIGHT AND FULL WITH POSITIVE ENERGY.
LET OUR MAGICK AND STRENGTH NEVER WANE
OR BE ECLIPSED BY DESTRUCTIVE FORCES
FROM WITHIN OR WITHOUT.

O MOTHER MOONLIGHT
PLEASE GUIDE US ON OUR LIFE'S JOURNEYS
AND THROUGH OUR PERSONAL TRANSFORMATIONS.
GRANT US INSPIRATION AND WHOLENESS.
I ASK THEE TO PLEASE BESTOW YOUR WISDOM
OF WHITE LIGHT UPON US.
ILLUMINATE THE TRUTH FOR US TO SEE,
HEAL US, AND REVEAL TO US
YOUR SACRED GODDESS POWER.

SO MOTE IT BE!

Give thanks to the Goddess in your own words, and then bring the ritual to a close by uncasting the circle in a counter-clockwise direction.

AUTUMN LEAF SPELL

Autumn Equinox

Write a secret wish upon a fallen leaf: Use a leaf with red colors for a wish pertaining to matters of love, sex, passion, or health; a gold-colored one for wishes involving money; a brown one for protection; a purple one for healing; an orange one for energy; a yellow one for confidence, attraction, or persuasion; a green one for fertility, success, or good luck.

Fold the leaf in half (or roll it up) and seal it with a kiss. Using the flame of a white candle, set the leaf on fire. As it burns, visualize your wish coming true for you and recite thrice the following incantation:

BURN, BURN, GIFT FROM THE TREE
MAKE THIS WISH COME TRUE FOR ME

HORNED GOD RITUAL

October 18

On the eighteenth day of October, many Wiccans and Neo-Pagans from around the world perform a special ceremony to pay homage to Cernunnos, the ancient Horned God who presides over hunting, fertility, and all wild animals.

Cernunnos symbolizes the male principle and is regarded by many as the consort of the Goddess.

I honor Him by lighting a dark green candle on my altar and reciting the following Pagan rhyme:

O GREAT HORNED GOD, TO THEE I SING
THIS SONG OF PRAISE FOR ALL YOU BRING:

FOR GENTLE BEASTS AND BIRDS SO FREE,
FOR FERTILE LANDS AND WOODLAND TREES.
YOU ARE THE GOD OF DARKEST NIGHT
AND BRINGER OF THE BRIGHTEST LIGHT.
THE EARTH IS YOUR KINGDOM,
THE SKY IS YOUR THRONE;
BY MANY NAMES YOU HAVE BEEN KNOWN.
ANCIENT AS TIME AND SPACE YOU ARE,
MAJESTIC AS THE SKY ABLAZE WITH STARS.
O GREAT HORNED GOD OF PAGAN LOVE,
MY HEART BEATS FOR YOU
LIKE A TREMBLING DOVE.

SO MOTE IT BE!

ALL HALLOWS' EVE (SAMHAIN)

October 31

Samhain is the most important of the eight Sabbats observed by Witches throughout the course of the year. It is a time of feasting on traditional Pagan foods (such as pumpkin pie and Cakes for the Dead), performing rituals to honor deceased love ones, and divining the future by various methods, both ancient and modern.

Many Witches look into the past, present, and future on this night by means of scrying (gazing) into crystal balls, magick-mirrors, or cauldrons of water on which a film of oil has been poured. Scrying is considered by most who follow the Old Religion to be the traditional Samhain form of divination; however, I like to be different and perform my Samhain divinations with the seeds from the pumpkins that I carve into jack-o'-lanterns.

Two of the ways in which to divine with pumpkin seeds are as follows: Holding a handful of pumpkin seeds (washed and thoroughly dried), ask thrice your question aloud and then recite the following incantation:

PUMPKIN SEEDS
PUMPKIN SEEDS
SPELL OUT THE ANSWER
THAT I NEED.

Cast the pumpkin seeds into the air and then study the position in which they fall. Often they will spell out one or more letters of the alphabet and/or numbers which can offer a clue. Sometimes they will create a symbolic pattern instead when they land on the ground or on the floor. This pattern, when properly interpreted, will give you the answer to your question.

For instance, if you asked if marriage was foreseen in your immediate future and the seeds you tossed formed a circular pattern (which would most likely symbolize a wedding ring), the answer can be interpreted as affirmative.

The second method of pumpkin seed divination is more general and calls for the seeds to be cast into a fire. If they do not crackle as they burn, this is not considered to be a favorable omen. However, if they do crackle, the omen is said to be very good. And the louder the seeds crackle as they burn, the *better* the omen!

In addition to performing divinations, many Witches employ various methods to communicate with the spirit world on Samhain night. Some of these methods include séances, Ouija boards, and spirit channeling.

Whichever method a Witch chooses, he or she should take care to first perform a spell of protection before engaging in spirit conjuration. This can be done by visualizing a circle of white light surrounding you and reciting the following incantation:

BE BANISHED ALL NEGATIVE ENERGIES,
ALL EVIL FORCES AND UNFRIENDLY ENTITIES
FROM THIS CIRCLE OF WHITE LIGHT.
GO NOW IN PEACE AND HARMING NONE.
ONLY THE SPIRITS WITH WHOM
I DESIRE COMMUNICATION
SHALL BE PERMITTED ENTRY.

I NOW CALL UPON THE ANCIENT
NATURE SPIRITS OF AIR
TO GUARD THIS CIRCLE
AND ENERGIZE IT WITH THE MAGICK
AND THE POWER OF THEIR ELEMENT.

I NOW CALL UPON THE ANCIENT
NATURE SPIRITS OF FIRE
TO GUARD THIS CIRCLE
AND ENERGIZE IT WITH THE MAGICK
AND THE POWER OF THEIR ELEMENT.

I NOW CALL UPON THE ANCIENT
NATURE SPIRITS OF WATER
TO GUARD THIS CIRCLE
AND ENERGIZE IT WITH THE MAGICK
AND THE POWER OF THEIR ELEMENT.

I NOW CALL UPON THE ANCIENT
NATURE SPIRITS OF EARTH
TO GUARD THIS CIRCLE
AND ENERGIZE IT WITH THE MAGICK
AND THE POWER OF THEIR ELEMENT.
SO MOTE IT BE!

The ancient art of scrying is a Samhain night tradition among the majority of modern-day Witches. (photo by Al B. Jackter)

Spirit Conjuration:

ON THIS SACRED NIGHT OF DARKNESS
WHEN THE VEIL IS THE THINNEST
AND THE CRONE REIGNS AS QUEEN,
TO THE SPIRIT OF (*name of deceased*)
AND TO (*repeat name of deceased*) ALONE
DO I OPEN THE INVISIBLE DOOR
THAT SEPARATES MY WORLD FROM YOURS
AND YOUR WORLD FROM MINE.
I SUMMON THEE NOW

O SPIRIT OF (*repeat name of deceased*)
INTO THIS CIRCLE OF LIGHT.
COME NOW WITH HASTE
AND HARMING NONE.
SO MOTE IT BE!

LOVE DIVINATION

December 1

The first day of December is a traditional time for young ladies in many parts of the world to perform a special love divination in order to discover who their future mates will be.

This is done with onion sprouts, and the official name for this method of divination is cromniomancy. It has been practiced since the earliest times; however, exactly how and where it originated remains a bit of a mystery.

If you are an unmarried woman (of any age) and desire to learn the name of the man destined to be your future lover or marriage mate, take some onions (as many as you wish) and upon each one, carve or write a different man's name as you recite the following magickal incantation:

ONION SPROUT REVEAL TO ME
THE NAME OF MY TRUE LOVE TO BE.

Place the onions near a fire and keep an eye on them over the next few days. The man whose name is on the onion that sprouts first will most likely be your true love, according to the divination.

Note: It seems that, according to many old books written about the divinatory arts, love divination by onion sprouts is traditionally performed by females; however, I personally see

no reason why this method cannot be used with successful results for single males who desire to discover the names of their future mates as well.

GOLDEN GODDESS PRAYER

Winter Solstice

On this night of the year, the hours of darkness are the longest, the flowers of spring and summer and the autumn leaves are long gone, and the Crone's spell of snow and ice is felt throughout much of the land.

The Winter Solstice is a Sabbat which celebrates the sun's rebirth (as the hours of daylight begin to slowly increase and the hours of night's darkness begin to slowly decrease).

The following Wiccan prayer is dedicated to the Goddess who guides us on our spiritual paths and reminds us that even in the darkness and bitter cold of winter, there is always an abundance of light and warmth within Her sacred circle of love.

Light a gold-colored candle on the center of your altar. As you gaze into its flickering flame, open your heart to the Goddess and recite the following Wiccan prayer:

GOLDEN GODDESS OF LOVE AND MIGHT,
ERASE THE SHADOWS OF THIS DARK NIGHT,
WARM THE COLD WITH BLESSINGS BRIGHT
AND GUIDE ME ON YOUR PATH OF LIGHT.

SO MOTE IT BE!

Chapter 7

THE MAGICK OF VERSE

It seems only appropriate that I should begin this chapter with a poem that I wrote in honor of the Goddess. It is called *A Pagan Rhyme*:

> *Water, Fire, Air, and Earth,*
> *Womb to life, death to rebirth.*
> *Our Great Wheel of the seasons turns,*
> *The mortal heart forever yearns.*
> *The sacred Sabbat candle burns,*
> *Within our souls its light sojourns.*
> *We all are children of the Goddess*
> *And to Her we shall return:*
> *Womb to life, death to rebirth,*
> *Water, Fire, Air, and Earth.*

A poem is a magickal creation, and the ability to "give birth" to one is, in my opinion, truly a special gift from the Goddess.

The connection between poetry and the Craft is one that dates back to olden times. Many spells, incantations, invocations, and sacred chants are wholly or partly made up of rhyming verses that translate into magickal poetry. Upon reading them, an individual (even one who does not consider him or herself to be a poet) often feels his or her soul touched in some way, even if it is merely a feeling of being blessed with inspiration. And when recited out loud, especially with the Wiccan art of creative visualization, poetry transforms into a powerful tool of spellcraft.

Such poetry can be utilized to invoke power, to express the beauty of one's love for the Goddess and the Horned God, and to honor the ancient Pagan deities that inspire, protect, and guide each and every one of us on our spiritual paths.

Poetry does not necessarily have to be written in rhyme in order to be magickal or powerful. Unrhymed poetry is just as effective; however, for reciting out loud during rituals and spellcastings, my personal preference is the rhyming verse, as it just seems to "flow" better. Rhyming poetry, for me at least, is also easier to memorize than unrhymed poetry, and it can easily be set to music and sung.

The ancient Druids (the priestly caste of the Celts) were known to be magickal bards, especially in the country of Wales. They celebrated in song and rhyme the great deeds of their heroes, and there is some evidence to support the theory that they may have been the first ones to practice the art of satire.

In old Irish mythology and folk legend, satire is a magickal rhyming curse that was believed to possess the power to bring on illness or even death to any enemy when recited.

Although modern Witches, Wiccans, Neo-Pagans, and all who understand and mind both the Wiccan Rede and the Law of Three would never think of utilizing the destructive magick of satire as a means of dealing with enemies (there are safer methods to employ without incurring any karmic repercussions), its place in occult history establishes a link between poetry and the magickal arts. Satire also provides an excellent example of the power which can be created by the simple act of rhyming words.

If poetry can be used magickally for negative purposes (such as the satire clearly demonstrates), it only stands to reason then that poetry can also be used magickally for positive purposes.

POETRY HEALING

In addition to bringing joy and satisfaction, the reading, writing, and reciting of poems (especially those of a Pagan and/or Goddess-honoring nature) can have a healing effect on the physical body, the mind, and especially the spiritual self. Like relaxing New Age music, poetry (when used properly) can help calm the nerves, stimulate the psyche, attract beneficial energy vibrations, and set the ideal mood for both magickal and meditative trance-work.

The first step in using poetry as a healing tool is to select a suitable poem. It is important to find one that embraces you with a pleasant feeling both during and after reading it.

I would not recommend using any poem, regardless of how well it may be written or even if it is considered to be a classic work, if it arouses any type of negative feeling, anger, anxiety, sadness, confusion, and so forth, as these are emotions that are not conducive to healing.

If you possess the gift of poetry, it is perfectly acceptable to compose your own healing poem, especially if the healing you plan on performing is for yourself. In this case a personally written poem would be greatly beneficial, as it would be empowered with your own magickal energies, spiritual vibrations, and intent.

After selecting (or composing) the poem that you feel is the right one to work with, the next step is to set the proper mood. This can be done by choosing an area in your home (or even outdoors) where it is quiet and you will not be disturbed in any way. It is a good idea to unplug the telephone. Light some white candles and some incense if you like, turn on some relaxing instrumental music, and turn the lights down low or completely off, depending on which you feel most comfortable with. Relax and clear your mind of all negative and unpleasant thoughts.

When you feel you are ready, begin reading the poem (or poems) you have selected, either out loud or to yourself, while visualizing the healing effects taking place. You may use any visualization method that feels right for you.

If you are working with a single poem, you may wish to repeat it several times until you begin to feel the healing energy. If you have access to a tape recorder, you may find it easier to record yourself or someone else reciting the poetry with relaxing music in the background and then play it back as you do your visualization.

If you are performing a healing on someone other than yourself, you may also consider combining massage techniques or reflexology with the poetry recital and visualization.

The following poem is one that I have written for my own personal healing rituals. I would like to share it with you in the hope that it may inspire you to write your own. You may also use it in your own healings. Feel free to add to it or change it around to suit your personal needs. Remember, the more of yourself that you add to your spellcraft, the more effective your magick will be!

> *Throes and woes,*
> *like clouds of darkness,*
> *fade away, fade away . . .*

Like grains of sand
on stormswept beaches,
wash away, wash away . . .

Burn in white light
as these words I recite
and blow away,
blow far away
like ashes in the wind:
the healing magick now begins.

Poetry healing can also be used to treat cats, dogs, and other animals. They may not understand the exact meaning of the words you are reciting (although I'm sure there are some cat-lovers and dog-lovers out there who would beg to differ!), but what is important is that the mellow tone of the voice that is produced when poetry is recited is capable of producing calming and healing effects on most animals. When poetry healing is combined with a loving, gentle caress, the effects are even greater.

A sick or injured animal will recover faster with a poetry healing. It will also help to relax an animal that is nervous, upset, or in the process of giving birth.

The most effective healing poetry for cats would naturally be poetry that is written about cats and expresses love for them. Select dog poems for dogs, horse poems for horses, and so forth. Of course you can always write your own poem in dedication to your beloved furry friend and use that.

To some individuals (especially nonpoets or those who do not have a close relationship with an animal), I'm sure this method may seem rather unorthodox, but nevertheless, it works with positive results nearly every time.

Poetry healing, whether for humans or animals, can be used any time one feels the need to perform it, regardless of the phase of the moon or whichever astrological sign it is positioned in. However, to get the most out of your magick, it is always a good idea to work in harmony with Lady Luna and her mystical lunar energies.

Therefore, if you are performing a healing when the moon is on the increase (waxing), I suggest incorporating this energy into your magick by visualizing a healthy condition being gained, strength improving, the healing process intensifying, and so on. Remember, when spellcasting during a waxing lunar phase, the key word to keep in mind is "increase."

If you are performing a healing when the moon is on the decrease (waning), visualize the disease or sickness as a dark cloud inside the body, and will it to fade away or be gradually consumed by the healing energy of white light. The power of will is very strong and can be used to help alleviate pain, destroy infections, etc. The key word to bear in mind during a waning moon is "decrease."

Changing your visualization method from increasing to decreasing and vice versa to correspond with the moon's phase may seem like a minor or unnecessary technicality, but it is actually a very important adjustment and one of the keys to performing successful, if not downright powerful, magick.

RHAPSODOMANCY

The use of poetry (including song lyrics) as a means of divination dates back to ancient times.

The formal name of this branch of the occult sciences is rhapsodomancy, which draws its name from the Greek words *rhapsodia*, meaning "rhapsody," and *mancy*, meaning "divination."

Rhapsodomancy is a form of bibliomancy (the art and practice of divination by books) and is believed to have originated in Greece and Rome, where the two most popular books used for this purpose were Homer's *Odyssey* and Virgil's *The Aenid*. Divination involving works by Homer was known as Homeric Lots, while Virgilian Lots was the name given to methods involving the works of Virgil. Both were typically performed in the following manner:

After special prayers or incantations were recited over the book, a specific question would be asked out loud. The book would then be opened at random and the first line that came into view would be interpreted as prophetic.

The basis for this unique method of divining was the belief that the gods or the all-knowing supernaturals of the spirit world, if choosing to offer their assistance, could reveal to mortals the answer to any question put forth to them. This was done by means of invisibly guiding the diviner's hands to open the book to the correct page containing the required indication. Of course if the man or woman who sought the help of the gods was not deemed to be worthy by them, they would furnish him or her with an incorrect reply or one that would bring a great deal of confusion to the mind.

Rhapsodomancy continues to be practiced in modern times. While some diviners prefer to adhere to the traditional method using the classic works of Homer and Virgil, just about any book of poetry or prose, classical or contemporary, can be employed with successful results.

As a diviner myself, I have found that poetry divination seems to work best when it is performed around midnight, especially when the moon is full. (It is also during this time when psychic abilities and magickal powers are believed to be at their peak.)

I usually begin my divination by lighting candles and incense, and then selecting the book of poetry which will be consulted. As I hold the book between my hands, allowing it to absorb my energies, I concentrate upon a specific question

Almost any book can be used for divination; however, many modern Witches favor the use of grimoires and collections of poetry. (Photo by Gerina Dunwich)

or on an important issue which is concerning me and for which I feel I need guidance. When I sense that the time is right, I recite the following magickal rhyme:

O MIGHTY AND ALL-KNOWING GUIDES
THE TRUTH I ASK THEE TO PROVIDE.
WITHIN THESE PAGES PRINTED AND BOUND
MAY THE ANSWER I NEED BE FOUND.
SO MOTE IT BE!

With my eyes closed and my mind focused on my question, I then open the book to whatever page feels right to me and place the index finger of my right hand at whatever place on the page that my finger feels most guided to. I open my eyes and interpret an answer from the line chosen at random. Once in a while the answer may at first appear abstract or vague, but usually after analyzing it a bit, the message suddenly becomes apparent.

Afterwards I always give sincere thanks to the spirit guides for their kind assistance. I do not believe in taking magickal favors, no matter how small, for granted.

Often a poetry divination will result in some sort of advice rather than a prediction revealed outright. If you receive any advice that you feel would be against your better judgment to follow, or if you are presented with any message that upsets you or makes you feel threatened in any way, close the book immediately, thank the spirits, and then end the divination for the rest of the evening. You might also at that point consider doing a positive energy ritual in which you visualize yourself surrounded by a protective circle of pure white light.

If when performing poetry divination you find the answers you are receiving to be consistantly incorrect or incoherent, it may be an indication that the time for divination is inauspicious. Stop and wait until later on or maybe even until the following day before resuming. If the same problem continues, I suggest that you try switching to a different book of poetry or prose. It is a good idea to experiment with several until you find the right one that harmonizes the best with your own personal energies.

RITUAL FOR POETIC INSPIRATION

I perform the following ritual almost every time I sit down to write a poem. (However, quite a few of my poems mysteriously come to me by way of dreams and some are channeled much in the same manner that messages from the spirit realm are received by spiritualist mediums, shamans, and trance channelers.)

I light white candles and incense, and then cast a clockwise circle in the divine names of the Goddess and the Horned God. (You may, if you wish, cast your circle in the name of a specific deity, particularly one who presides over the art of poetry or is a patron of poets. The following Pagan goddesses and gods are all associated with poetry: Apollo, Benten, Bragi, Brigid, Hathor, Odin, Orpheus, Thoth, Vainemuine, Woden, and Xochipillo.)

After the circle has been cast, I sit comfortably in the center of it with my pencil and pad of paper at hand. I clear my mind of any negative thoughts and my heart of any negative feelings. I begin to visualize a glowing circle of white light surrounding me and I recite the following incantation:

I BLESS THIS CIRCLE IN THE DIVINE NAME OF THE GODDESS AND IN THE DIVINE NAME OF THE HORNED GOD.

MAY THIS CIRCLE BECOME A SACRED SPACE IN WHICH MAGICKAL VERSE IS BORN.

LET ALL NEGATIVE VIBRATIONS AND INHIBITIONS BE DISPELLED AT ONCE, AND MAY I BE DEEMED WORTHY TO RECEIVE THE BLESSING OF ABUNDANT POETIC INSPIRATION.

THANK YOU, GODDESS AND GOD.
SO MOTE IT BE.

As this chapter began with one of my Pagan poems, so shall it close with one:

SEASONS CHANGE

(Onward We Flow)

Seasons change,
the Wheel turns—
and onward we flow,
*   onward we flow,*
like a mountain stream
that dances so free
and fairy-crystal bright.

Children of the Goddess Earth:
we never change
or stay the same;
of many faces we are made
yet we are all as one.

Onward we flow,
onward we flow,
like the molten gifts
of the Volcano Goddess
that meander their way
to the waiting sea.

The sacred ring
of life and death
forever turns;
it brightly burns
like a supernatural
spinning wheel
of fire within our souls.

Seasons change—
day follows day
and the sun rises and sets,
    rises and sets,
like a fire-dancer
in an endless ballet
set to Nature's sacred
    symphony.

And onward we flow
like the crimson blood
that connects us
to life, so precious
and to the ancient
Woman/Goddess cycles
ruled by the moon and by time . . .

. . . and all beginnings
must have an end;
and from all endings,
as it always has been
and it always will be,
a new beginning shall
    emerge.

Seasons change—
we shine,
we fade,
yet onward we flow,
    onward we flow. . . .

Chapter 8

GLOSSARY
OF THE WICCAN CRAFT

ALTAR: Any table or raised structure on which, during rituals and spellcastings, candles and incense are burned, tools of magick are kept, and offerings of any kind are made to the Goddess and/or the Horned God. The arrangement of altars varies from Witch to Witch and coven to coven; however, the usual items found on most Wiccan altars include candles, a pentacle, chalice, salt, incense, bell, athame, and a Goddess and/or Horned God symbol. Nearly any piece of furniture with a flat surface can be used as an altar, and with a little imagination, outdoor altars can be easily made out of such things as garden benches, tree stumps, and large stones with flat tops.

AMULET: A consecrated object (usually a small, colored stone, or a piece of metal inscribed with runes or other magickal symbols) that possesses the power to draw love

128 ◆

A WITCH'S ALTAR. From left to right: The black bag in front of the cat gargoyle contains a deck of Tarot cards for divination. Next to it is a chalice for water, a candelabra, a container of salt, a consecrated athame (ritual dagger), and an old wooden box for holding amulets, talismans, and other magickal objects. To the right of the altar is a besom (a Witch's straw broom traditionally used for "sweeping away" negative energy vibrations from the magick circle). (Photo by Gerina Dunwich)

or good luck, among other things. Amulets are also used to protect against threatening influences, evil, and misfortune.

ATHAME: A ritual knife with a double-edged blade, used by Witches (and other practitioners of the magickal arts) to cast magick circles and to store and direct energy during rituals.

BELL: A hollow, metallic instrument, usually cup-shaped with a flared opening, which emits a tone when struck by a clapper suspended within or by a separate stick or hammer. Bells have been used by nearly all cultures throughout history as magickal talismans, fertility charms, summons to a deity, and as instruments for sacred music and religious rituals of widely varying beliefs. Many modern-day Witches use a consecrated bell as an altar tool to signal the beginning and/or close of a ritual or Sabbat.

BESOM: A straw broom used by Witches in certain Wiccan ceremonies such as Handfasting and the Sabbat of Candlemas. Although the broom has always been associated with Witches, it was never actually used for flying. Instead, Witches practicing sympathetic magick (which works on the basic principle that like produces like) would straddle the broom and jump up and down in order to show the crops how high to grow.

BEWITCHMENT: The act of gaining power over another person by means of white or black magick; the act of casting a spell over a man, woman, child, or animal.

BINDING: A magickal spell, often involving the tying of knots on a cord, and performed to control the actions of another or to render a sorcerer or sorceress magickally powerless. Bindings are used by some Wiccans, usually for the purpose of preventing evil, negativity, or disaster of some kind from occurring, and also to put an end to the harm caused by gossips, troublemakers, and those who commit crimes. Interestingly, there exists a controversy among Wiccans over how ethical the casting of bindings are. Some Wiccans feel that such spells violate the Wiccan Rede, while others feel that they are perfectly acceptable when warranted, especially if the binding is directed at a situation rather than at a specific person.

BINDRUNES: A magickal talisman, usually made from metal or wood, and inscribed or painted with two or more different rune symbols which are superimposed upon one another in an aesthetically pleasing fashion. Bindrunes are sometimes placed on ritual tools (such as the blade and/or handle of a Witch's athame), candles, and jewelry.

BOLLINE: A white-handled knife with a sharp blade used by Witches to harvest sacred herbs, cut wooden wands, slice bread, and carve magickal symbols in candles and talismans.

BOOK OF SHADOWS: A secret diary of magickal spells and potion recipes kept by an individual Witch or a coven. In certain Wiccan traditions, a Witch's Book of Shadows must be burned in the event of his or her death in order to protect the secrets of the Craft.

BUNE WAND: An old Scottish nickname given to the legendary Witches' broomstick, or any object supposedly used by Witches as a flying instrument.

BURIN: A special engraving tool used by Witches (and other practitioners of the magickal arts) to mark names or symbols ritually on athames, swords, bells, and other magickal tools.

CAKES FOR THE DEAD: In the country of Belgium, it was once a popular Samhain (Halloween) custom for families to prepare special, small white cakes or cookies known as "Cakes for the Dead." One would be consumed for each deceased loved one being honored, and it was believed that the more cakes a person ate, the more he or she would be blessed by the spirits.

CANDLE MAGICK: A form of sympathetic magick that uses colored candles to represent the people and things at which its spells are directed. Each color symbolizes a different attribute, influence, and emotion. There are also different astral colors for each of the twelve signs of the zodiac.

CAULDRON: A small, black, cast-iron pot used by Witches that symbolically combines the influences of the four ancient elements, represents the womb of the Goddess, and is used for

A small hanging cauldron used for holding magickal herbs and also for burning incense. (Photo by Gerina Dunwich)

A large cauldron used for healing rituals and various fire-spells. (Photo by Gerina Dunwich)

various purposes, including brewing potions, burning incense, and holding charcoal or herbs.

CENSER: A fireproof incense burner used in magickal rituals, and symbolic of the ancient element of Air.

CERNUNNOS: Celtic horned nature-god of wild animals, hunting, and fertility, "Lord of All Living Creatures," and consort of the Great Mother. He is depicted as a hirsute man with antlers and hoofs, and his name literally means "the Horned One." In ancient times, he was worshipped in Britain and in Celtic Europe. As a Neo-Pagan god, he is often worshipped by Wiccans of the Gardnerian tradition.

CHALICE: A sacred cup or goblet used by Witches to hold consecrated water or wine, and to symbolize the ancient element of Water.

CHARM: A highly magickal object that works like an amulet or talisman; a magickal song or incantation which is often chanted over an amulet or talisman to consecrate it and charge it with magickal energy.

CINGULUM: In certain traditions of Wicca, a consecrated cord (nine feet long and red) used by Witches when dancing to raise power. Nine knots on the cord are used for storing built-up power for future magickal use. To release the power, the knots must be untied in the exact order in which they were tied.

CONE OF POWER: The ritual act of visualizing energy in the form of a spiral light rising from the circle, and directing it toward a specific goal or task.

CONSECRATION: The act, process, or ceremony of making something sacred; the ritual use of water and salt to exorcise negative energies and/or evil influences from ritual tools, circles, and so forth.

COUNTERCHARM: A powerful magickal charm that is used to either neutralize or reverse the effects of another charm or spell.

COUNTERSPELL: A powerful magickal spell or incantation that neutralizes or reverses the effects of another spell or charm.

COVEN: A group of Witches, traditionally thirteen in number, who gather together to work magick and perform ceremonies at Sabbats and Esbats. A *COVENER* is a man or woman who is a member of a coven, and a *COVENSTEAD* is the place where a coven holds its regular meetings.

COWAN: Among Witches, a person who is not a Witch.

THE CRAFT: Witchcraft, Wicca, the Old Religion, the practice of folk magick.

DEOSIL: A word used by Wiccans to mean clockwise. In spells and rituals, deosil movement symbolizes life and positive energy.

DIANIC: A Wiccan tradition or type of coven that worships only the Goddess or accords the Horned God secondary status to the Goddess. Dianic feminist Wicca encourages female leadership and involves its practitioners in many feminist issues. Although some covens of the Dianic tradition include both female and male members, many of them exclude men, and some are lesbian-oriented.

DIVINATION: The occult science, art, and practice of discovering the unknown and foretelling events of the future by interpreting omens or by various methods such as Tarot cards, dice, crystal balls, Ouija boards, astrology, and so forth.

DRAWING DOWN THE MOON: The ritual invocation of the Goddess spirit-force into the High Priestess of a coven by the High

Priest who uses his male polarity to conjure forth the divine essence in the female polarity of the High Priestess. During this modern ritual (also known as "Calling Down the Moon"), the High Priestess enters a trance-like altered state of consciousness, and draws the power of the Goddess into herself. The High Priestess then functions as a channel of the Goddess or as the Goddess incarnate in the circle until it has been uncast.

DRAWING DOWN THE SUN: The ritual invocation of the Horned God spirit-force into the High Priest of a coven by the High Priestess who uses her female polarity to conjure forth the divine essence in the male polarity of the High Priest. During this modern ritual (also known as "Calling Down the Sun" or "Drawing Down the Horned God"), the High Priest enters a trance-like altered state of consciousness, and draws the power of the Horned God into himself. The High Priest then functions as a channel of the Horned God or as the Horned God incarnate within the circle until it has been uncast.

EKE-NAME: A Witch's secret name, also known as a Witchname. Many Witches take on one or more secret names to signify their rebirth and new life within the Craft. Eke-names are most sacred and are used only among brothers and sisters of the same path. When a Witch takes on a new name, he or she must be careful to choose one that harmonizes in one way or another with numerological name-numbers, birth-numbers, or runic numbers. A well-chosen name vibrates with that individual and directly links him or her to the Craft.

ELEMENTALS: Spirit-creatures that personify the qualities of the four ancient elements. Salamanders are the elemental spirits of Fire; Undines are the elemental spirits of Water; Sylphs are the elemental spirits of Air; and Gnomes are the elemental spirits of Earth.

ELEMENTAL SIGNS: The signs of Fire, Water, Air, and Earth. Fire is the symbol of energy, individuality, and identity; Water is the symbol of life, love, and spirit; Air is the symbol of the mind; and Earth is the symbol of strength and fertility.

ENCHANTMENT: Another word for magick; the act of bewitching or casting a spell.

ESBAT: A regular meeting of a coven that is held during the full moon at least thirteen times a year. At an esbat, coven members exchange ideas, discuss problems, perform special rites, work magick and healing, and give thanks and/or request help from the Goddess and the Horned God.

FAMILIAR: A Witch's pet. In medieval Witchcraft and folklore, the familiar was an attendant spirit that appeared in the form of a cat, lizard, hare, toad, or other small animal to aid a Witch in the practice of magick.

THE GODDESS: The female aspect of the Divine; the consort of the Horned God (the male aspect of the Divine); and the main deity honored and invoked by many Wiccans. Worship of the Goddess has been traced back as far as primitive times and She has been known by thousands of names throughout various cultures, past and present, from around the world.

GRAY MAGICK: The art and practice of magick that is neither totally white nor totally black; magick that combines elements of both white and black; or white magick that borders on being black magick, but is not necessarily performed with evil or malicious intent. Love spells that are of a manipulative nature, a death spell to end the long and painful suffering of a terminally ill loved one, and a self-defense spell that returns a curse to its sender, are several examples of gray magick.

GREAT RITE: Ritual sexual intercourse which is performed either actually or symbolically as a sublime religious experience. This major male/female "polarity" ritual (also known as the "Sacred Marriage") is often enacted at major Sabbats (especially Samhain) by the High Priestess and the High Priest of a coven who draw down into themselves the spirit of the Goddess and the Horned God, respectively, and experience a divine union that is both spiritual and physical. In certain Wiccan traditions (such as Gardnerian), the Great Rite is performed as part of the Third Degree Initiation, which promotes a Witch to the highest of the three grades of the Craft.

The performing of the Great Rite is by no means a mandatory requirement in the Wiccan craft, nor is it merely just an excuse to indulge in sexual pleasures under the guise of religion. It is in fact an extremely serious ritual as it releases an enormous amount of power which is directed with magickal intent. It is traditionally performed (in private) only by a consenting High Priestess and High Priest, and never sexually involves other members of the coven. It is also important to point out that in this age of fatal sexually transmitted diseases, many Wiccans choose to perform the Great Rite in symbolic fashion only. This calls for the High Priest to plunge the blade of his athame (symbol of the phallus and male energy) into the High Priestess' wine-filled chalice (symbol of the vagina and female energy).

GREEN WITCH: A nickname for a female or male Witch who is skilled in the art of wortcunning. The herb magick practiced by a Green Witch is called "the Green Arts" or "Green Magick"; the use of medicinal herbs is known as "Green Healing."

GRIMOIRE: A magickal workbook containing various spells, formulas, rituals, and incantations; any collection of magickal spells and formulas. One of the most famous of all grimoires is the medieval *Key of Solomon*, which contains conjurations, prayers, detailed pentacles for each of the planets, and detailed commentaries on the nature of spirits invoked in ceremonial magick, Witchcraft, and necromancy.

HALLOWEEN: See SAMHAIN.

HANDFASTING: A Wiccan betrothal ceremony in which the hands of the bride and groom are tied together with a consecrated knotted cord to signify that they have been joined together in matrimonial union. A handfasting may be performed as either a legally binding wedding or as a nonlegally binding spiritual commitment rite.

HANDPARTING: A Wiccan ceremony that dissolves the marriage partnership of a man and a woman who are nonlegally married to each other.

HORNED GOD: The consort of the Goddess and the symbol of male sexuality. The Horned God in many Wiccan traditions is usually identified with the Greek nature-god Pan, or Cernunnos, the Celtic lord of wild animals.

KARMA: The law of cause-and-effect that applies to all of our actions and their consequences in this life or in future incarnations.

LIBATION: Water or wine which is ritually poured on an altar, on the ground, or on a sacred fire as an offering to the Goddess, the Horned God, or other deity.

LOVE MAGICK: Any form of magick which is performed by a Witch or other practitioner or magick during the proper phase of the moon to either attract, strengthen, or restore love. Love potions (also known as philtres) and love charms are two popular methods of love magick which have been used worldwide since ancient times.

LOVE POTION: An herbal aphrodisiac used in magickal spells with incantations to arouse love or sexual passion; a philtre.

LOW MAGICK: The magickal arts of Witchcraft, spellcraft, hex-craft, and hoodoo which utilize herbs, amulets, wax images, and other simple material objects in conjunction with incantations and visualizations to bring about a desired result; the folk magick of rural populations often performed for a fee; the casting of spells for either good or evil, as opposed to High Magick (also known as "Ceremonial Magick") which is performed for the supreme purpose of union with the Divine. Low Magick is often referred to as "Natural Magick."

MAGICK: The art, science, and practice of producing "super-natural" effects, causing change to occur in conformity, and controlling events in Nature with will. As a tool of Witch-craft, the old spelling of the word with a final "K" is used to distinguish it from the magic of conjuring and illusion which has nothing to do with ceremonial workings or the magickal states of consciousness produced by ritual.

MAGICK SQUARES: Powerful magickal talismans made from rows of numbers or letters of the alphabet arranged so that the words may read horizontally or vertically as palindromes, and the numbers total the same when added up in either direction.

MOJO BAG: A small leather or flannel bag filled with a variety of magickal items such as herbs, stones, feathers, bones, and so forth, and carried or worn as a charm to attract or dispel certain influences.

MOON: In Witchcraft and Wicca, the sacred symbol of the Goddess and also a symbol of magick, fertility, and the secret powers of Nature.

NEO-PAGANISM: The practice of modern-day Paganism; a contemporary and eclectic movement that aims to revive pre-Christian nature religions, Goddess worship, and mystery traditions by infusing them with modern concepts.

OFFERING: In Wicca, Witchcraft and magick, a presentation made to the Goddess, the Horned God, or other deity as an act of religious worship or sacrifice. (See LIBATION.)

THE OLD ONES: The gods of the Old Religion, also known as "The Ancients." In Wicca, all aspects of the Goddess and Her consort, the Horned God.

THE OLD RELIGION: Another name for Witchcraft.

PAGAN: A word stemming from the Latin *paganus*, meaning a "country dweller" and used derogatorily by the Church to describe a follower of the Old Religion, or any person who was not a Christian, Jew, or Moslem; a follower of Wicca and other polytheistic religions.

PENTACLE: (1) The symbol of the five-pointed star (often within a circle) which represents the four ancient elements of Air, Fire, Water, and Earth, surmounted by the Spirit. The pentacle symbol is used by many Witches in spells and magickal ceremonies. (2) A flat wood, wax, metal, or clay disc bearing the motif of the mystical five-pointed star, and used in magickal ceremonies and spells to represent feminine energy and the ancient element of Earth. It is known also as a "magician's pentacle" and a "Pentacle of Solomon."

PENTAGRAM: Any written or drawn pentacle symbol, including both invoking and banishing pentagrams which are drawn in the air with an athame or sword.

PHILTRE: An herbal aphrodisiac used in magickal spells with incantations to arouse love or sexual desire. Also known as "love potions," philtres have been used by Witches since ancient times and have consisted of many different herbal ingredients. They are often put in foods or drinks and work the best when prepared and used on a Friday (the day of the week most sacred to Venus, the ancient goddess of love) or at the time of the month when the moon is positioned in the astrological sign of Taurus.

POPPET: A specially prepared herb-stuffed cloth doll that is used in sympathetic magick rituals to represent the person at whom the spell is directed.

POTION: An herbal tea or brew used by Witches in magickal or healing rituals. In order to work properly, a potion must be prepared during the appropriate phase of the moon and made with herbal ingredients possessing the correct magickal properties. Potions are traditionally brewed in cauldrons and are used in all facets of the magickal arts. Potions concocted for the workings of love magick are often called "philtres."

PRACTICAL MAGICK: Witchcraft, folk-magick; magick that is concerned with things of the Earth, harmony with Nature, seasons, and cycles. Unlike ceremonial magick which requires complicated rituals and elaborate (and often expensive) ritual tools and ceremonial clothing, practical magick is performed with the aid of simple, common implements.

REINCARNATION: The repeated birth of the same soul in different physical bodies. Reincarnation is an ancient and mystical belief that is part of many religions, including Wicca, and is commonly associated with the concept of spiritual evolution.

RITUAL: A religious or magickal ceremony characterized by symbolic attire and formalized behavior, and designed to produce desired effects such as spiritual illumination or supernatural power, or to invoke a specific deity.

RUNES: Letters of a secret magickal alphabet that spell words of power and are widely used in magick and divination. Runes can be written, painted, or carved into ritual tools, magicians' robes, talismans, amulets, ceremonial jewelry, and other things to charge the object with power. They also can be marked on flat wooden sticks or stones and used to divine future events or unknown circumstances.

SABBAT: One of the eight Wiccan festivals; the gathering of Witches to celebrate at specific times of the year the transitions in the seasons. The four major Sabbats are: Candlemas, Beltane, Lammas, and Samhain. The four minor ones are Spring Equinox, Summer Solstice, Autumnal Equinox, and Winter Solstice.

SAMHAIN: One of the four Grand Sabbats, also known as Halloween, and celebrated on October 31. Samhain is the most important of all the Witches' Sabbats. It is the ancient Celtic/Druid New Year, and also the time when spirits of deceased loved ones and friends are honored. At one time in history, many believed that it was the night when the dead returned to walk among the living. The divinatory arts of scrying and runecasting are Samhain traditions among many Wiccans.

SCEPTER: A wand used by Witches (and other practitioners of the magickal arts) in certain magickal spells and rituals.

SCRYING: The art and practice of interpreting the future, past, or present from images seen while gazing into a crystal ball, candle flame, pool of water, or gazing mirror; crystal-gazing; mirror-gazing.

SEAL OF SOLOMON: A hexagram consisting of two interlocking triangles, one facing up and the other facing down. It symbolizes the human soul and is used by many Witches in spells and rituals involving spirit communication, wisdom, purification, and/or the strengthening of psychic powers.

SIMPLE: This is an archaic word used by Witches of old to mean a plant of medicine or the medicine obtained from it. Simples, which are a mainstay of many folk healers and country Witches, are usually very mild and indigenous plants. They are used completely by themselves to prevent or treat disease.

SKYCLAD: A term used by Witches to mean ritual nudity (clad only by the sky). Skyclad worshipping is common among certain traditions of Wicca (such as the Alexandrians and strict Gardnerians) and is carried out in the belief that nudity brings a Witch closer to the divine forces of Nature and equalizes all members of a coven. However, many Wiccans (especially those who work with others in a circle) choose not to worship skyclad as they personally feel more comfortable and nonetheless closer to Nature and equality wearing ceremonial robes or even everyday attire.

SMUDGING: The burning of incense or an herb bundle to drive away negative forces and to purify the space in which magick is to be performed. The most common herb used for smudging is sage.

SOLITARY: A name used for the type of Witch who, either by circumstances or by his or her own choice, practices the Craft without belonging to a coven.

SPELL: An incantational formula; a Wiccan prayer; a nonreligious magickal ritual performed by a Witch or other practitioner of the magickal arts.

SPELLCRAFT: The performing of magickal spells in any form for either good or evil; magick in general; the art and practice of folk-magick common among rural populations; the art and practice of sorcery (any form of black magick, especially medieval style, that is performed with evil intent).

SUFFUMIGATIONS: Magickal incenses made from herbs and burned by Witches and magicians to attract spirits and enable them to materialize. Suffumigations are used in ceremonial magick, séances, and necromancy.

TALISMAN: A man-made object of any shape or material charged with magickal properties to bring good luck, fertility, and ward off evil. To formally charge a talisman with power, it must first be inscribed and then consecrated. Inscribing the talisman with a sun sign, moon sign, birthdate, Runic name, or other magickal symbol personalizes it and gives it purpose.

THREEFOLD LAW: In Wicca, the belief that if one does good, he or she will get it back threefold in the same lifetime. Whatever harm one does to others is also returned threefold. (It is also known as Triple Karma.)

THURIBLE: A shallow, three-legged dish used in magickal workings as an incense burner.

TRIPLE GODDESS: A Goddess trinity having three different aspects and three different names, usually corresponding to the three lunar phases. In Her waxing phase, She is the Maiden. In Her full moon phase, She is the Mother. In Her waning or dark moon phase, She is the Crone of wisdom, death, and darkness.

UNCTION: The act of anointing a person or ritual tool with an herbal ointment or oil as part of a consecration, magickal ceremony, or healing ritual. Unctions are commonly performed in the spells and rituals of Wicca Craft. The term "unction" is also used for a balm, oil, or salve.

UNGUENT: A special ointment or salve used by Witches to promote healing and to induce astral projections and psychic dreams. Also known as "flying ointment" and "sorcerer's grease." In the Middle Ages, unguents containing various hallucinogenic ingredients were believed to give a Witch the powers of flight, invisibility, and transformation.

VISUALIZATION: In magick, the process of forming mental images of needed goals during rituals and spellcasting. Also called creative visualization and magickal visualization.

WAND: A stick used to trace circles, draw magickal symbols on the ground, invoke or conduct spiritual energy, and stir cauldron brews. The wand is the emblem of power. It represents the element of Air and is sacred to all Pagan deities.

WARLOCK: A word stemming from the Old English WAER-LOGA, meaning an "oath-breaker" and used derogatorily by the Church as a name for a male Witch. However, in Wicca, the word warlock is seldom, if ever, used. Both male and female practitioners of the Craft are called Witches.

WATCHTOWERS: Also known as the Directions or the Quarters, these are the four directional points at the perimeter of a magick circle to which each of the four spirits of the elements are called as guardians during the beginning of a ritual.

An old woodcut showing two Witches performing weatherworking magick to make rain. (Stock Montage, Inc.)

WEATHERWORKING: The art and practice of controlling atmospheric conditions by means of magick, prayer, or supernatural power; magickal control of the weather, most commonly used to make or stop rain.

WICCA: An alternative name for modern Witchcraft; a Neo-Pagan nature religion with spiritual roots in Shamanism, having one main tenet: the Wiccan Rede.

WICCAN REDE: A simple and benevolent moral code of Wiccans expressed as follows: "Eight words the Wiccan Rede fulfills; An' it harm none, do what ye will."

WIDDERSHINS: A word used by Wiccans to mean counterclockwise. This motion symbolizes negative magickal purposes and is mainly used to uncast the circle at the end of a ritual.

WITCH: Any individual, male or female, who practices Witchcraft; a Wiccan; one who worships the gods of the Old Religion.

WITCH BOTTLE: A glass bottle or jar which is filled with a variety of objects, charged with magickal power, and used for either good or evil. For example, a Witch bottle used in the art of love magick might contain such items as a lock of hair from the man or woman whose affections are desired, rose petals, heart-shaped candles, love amulets, Venus-ruled herbs, and other love-related goodies. After a Witch bottle has been filled, it is usually capped tightly and sealed with wax from an appropriately colored and/or scented candle. A magickal incantation is recited over the bottle and then it is either buried in the ground or hidden in some secret place until the Witch who cast the spell decides to break it, usually by smashing the bottle when the moon is in a waning phase, or by emptying its contents into a moving body of water.

WITCH HOLE: In the arts of magick and sorcery, a small hole which is dug in the ground (or in a flower pot) during the proper phase of the moon, filled with a variety of magickal objects, and then covered with dirt as part of a spell for either good or evil.

WITCHCRAFT: The Old Religion; the Craft of the Wise; the practice of folk religion that combines magick, Nature worship, divination, and herbalism with bits and pieces of various pre-Christian religious beliefs, notably those of the Druids and the ancient Egyptians.

WORTCUNNING: The knowledge and use of the secret healing and magickal properties of herbs; a word used by folk healers, Witches, and Wiccans of all traditions to mean the practice of herbalism. Wortcunning has been associated with the Old Religion since ancient times.

RESOURCES FOR THE MODERN WITCH

The following listings are of mail order companies across the United States, Canada, and England that sell herbs, candles, ritual tools, occult books, New Age gifts, gemstones, and other items of interest to Wiccans, Witches, and Neo-Pagans. They are listed in alphabetical order, and each one (as far as I know) currently offers a *free* catalogue. (IMPORTANT: If a *symbol appears after the name of the mail order company, this indicates that a self-addressed stamped envelope is required in order to have a free catalogue sent to you.)

NOTE: For a *complete* resource guide to Wiccan/Pagan organizations, churches, publishers, magickal and metaphysical retail and mail order outlets, and a who's who of the Wiccan community, please read my book, *The Wicca Sourcebook* (Citadel Press, 1996).

ABYSS DISTRIBUTION
48 Chester Road, Dept. WIG
Chester, Massachusetts 01011
(413) 623-2155; Fax: (413)
623-2156

AUNT AGATHA'S OCCULT
EMPORIUM
P.O. Box 64043
RPO Clark Road
Coquitlam, British Columbia
V3J 7V6
Canada
Fax: (604) 931-3874

BELL, BOOK, AND CANDLE
5886 Rocky Point
Long Island, New York, 11778

THE CRYSTAL PORTAL
P.O. Box 1934
Upper Marlboro, Maryland
  20773
(301) 952-9470

THE CRYSTAL ROSE*
P.O. Box 8416
Minneapolis, Minnesota 55408
(612) 488-3715

DRAGONS OF THE HEART
  DESIGNS
P.O. Box 367
Snowflake, Arizona 85937
(800) 439-2638

EARTH MAGIC
  PRODUCTIONS
2166 Broadway
New York, New York 10024
(800) 662-8634

EYE OF THE DAY
P.O. Box 21261
Boulder, Colorado 80308
(800) 717-3307

FENG SHUI WAREHOUSE
(800) 399-1599

GOLDEN ISIS*
P.O. Box 525
Fort Covington, New York
  12937

HALLORAN SOFTWARE
P.O. Box 75713
Los Angeles, California 90075
(800) SEA-GOAT; (818) 501-
  6515

HOURGLASS CREATIONS*
492 Breckenridge Street
Buffalo, New York 14213

ISLE OF AVALON
(800) 700-ISLE; (714) 646-
  4213

JANE IRIS DESIGNS
P.O. Box 608
Graton, California 95444

LLEWELLYN'S NEW
  WORLDS OF MIND
  AND SPIRIT
(800) THE-MOON

LUNATRIX*
P.O. Box 800482
Santa Clarita, California 91380

MAGICKAL CHILDE
35 W. 19th Street
New York, New York 10011
(212) 242-7182

METATOOLS
Box 8027
Santruce, Puerto Rico 00910

MOONSCENTS AND
MAGICKAL BLENDS
P.O. Box 381588
Cambridge, Massachusetts 02238
(800) 368-7417

MYSTERIA PRODUCTS
P.O. Box 1147
Arlington, Texas 76004

MYSTERIES
9 Monmouth Street
London, WC2
England
Phone: 01-240-3688

MYTHIC IMAGES*
P.O. Box 982
Ukiah, California 95482
(707) 485-7787

NEMETON*
P.O. Box 1542
Ukiah, California 95482
(707) 463-1432

PAN'S FOREST HERB
COMPANY
411 Ravens Road
Port Townsend, Washington
98368

ROSEWYND'S SIMPLES*
453 Proctor Road
Manchester, New Hampshire
03109

RUNES AND BINDRUNES*
P.O. Box 364
Dania, Florida 33004

SACRED ROSE
P.O. Box 331389
Fort Worth, Texas 76163

THE SAGE GARDEN
P.O. Box 144
Payette, Idaho 83661
(208) 454-2026

SALAMANDER ARMOURY*
15258 Lakeside Street
Sylmar, California 91342
(818) 362-5339

SHAPERS OF FANTASY
P.O. Box 5294
North Hollywood, California
91616

THE SORCERER'S
APPRENTICE
2103 Adderbury Circle
Madison, Wisconsin 53711
(608) 271-7591

WIDENING HORIZONS
21713-B N.E. 141st Street
Woodinville, Washington 98072
(206) 869-9810; Fax: (206)
869-1821

ZEPHYR SERVICES
1900 Murray Avenue
Pittsburgh, Pennsylvania 15217
(800) 533-6666; (412) 422-
6600

WICCAN/PAGAN ORGANIZATIONS

CHURCH OF ALL WORLDS
P.O. Box 1542
Ukiah, California 95482
(707) 463-1432

CIRCLE SANCTUARY
P.O. Box 219
Mount Horeb, Wisconsin
53572
(608) 924-2216

COVENANT OF THE
GODDESS
P.O. Box 1226
Berkeley, California 94701

EARTHSPIRIT
P.O. Box 365
Medford, Massachusetts 02155
(617) 395-1023; Fax: (617)
396-5066

FREE SPIRIT ALLIANCE
P.O. Box 25242
Baltimore, Maryland 21229
(301) 604-6049

NEW WICCAN CHURCH
P.O. Box 162046
Sacramento, California 95816

OUR LADY OF
ENCHANTMENT
P.O. Box 1366
Nashua, New Hampshire 03061
(603) 880-7237

PAGAN EDUCATIONAL
NETWORK
P.O. Box 1364
Bloomington, Indiana 47402

THE PAGAN POETS
SOCIETY/
NORTH COUNTRY WICCA
P.O. Box 264
Bombay, New York 12914

THE PAGAN FEDERATION
Box BM 7097
London, WC1N 3XX
England

REFORMED
  CONGREGATION
  OF THE GODDESS
P.O. Box 6677
Madison, Wisconsin 53716
(608) 244-0072

WHEEL OF WISDOM
  SCHOOL
c/o GOLDEN ISIS
P.O. Box 525
Fort Covington, New York
  12937

WICCAN/PAGAN PRESS
  ALLIANCE (W.P.P.A.)
P.O. Box 1392
Mechanicsburg, Pennsylvania
  17055

WISE WOMAN CENTER
P.O. Box 64
Woodstock, New York 12498

WICCAN/PAGAN PUBLICATIONS

CIRCLE NETWORK NEWS
P.O. Box 219
Mount Horeb, Wisconsin
  53572

GOLDEN ISIS MAGAZINE
P.O. Box 525
Fort Covington, New York
  12937

THE GREEN EGG
P.O. Box 1542
Ukiah, California 95482

MAGICAL BLEND
P.O. Box 11303
San Francisco, California 94101

SAGE WOMAN
P.O. Box 641
Point Arena, California 95468

A CALENDAR OF THE SACRED DAYS OF THE YEAR

The following is a calendar of the sacred days of the year, listing the dates on which many Pagan gods and goddesses from various cultures are honored.

JANUARY

1   Janus, the Three Fates, Bertha (German goddess), the Morrigan the Parcae, and all Japanese household gods.
2   Isis and Inanna (Sumerian Queen of Heaven).
3   Dionysus, the Deer Mothers (Native American spirit-goddesses).
4   The Korean god who rules Ursa Major.
6   Kore.
7   Sekhmet.
8   Babo, Freya, Justicia (Roman goddess of justice).
11 Carmenae (Roman nymphs of prophecy), Juturno.
12 The Lares (Roman household gods), Frigg (the chief goddess of Old England).
13 Tiu (an ancient Teutonic chief god and ruler of the year).
14 Surya (Indian god of the sun).
16 Concordia, Betoro Bromo (Indonesian god of fire).
17 Felicitas (Roman goddess of good fortune).
18 Zao Jun (Chinese kitchen-god).
19 Thor (Norse god of thunder and lightning).
21 Yngona (Danish goddess).

22 The Muses.

23 Hathor (Egyptian cow-headed goddess).

24 Ekeko (Aymara Indian god of prosperity).

25 All ancient gods and goddesses of Sweden.

27 Ishtar (Babylonian goddess of love and war).

29 Irene.

30 Pax (Roman goddess of peace).

31 The Valkyries, the Norns, Kuan Yin (Chinese goddess of healing and mercy).

FEBRUARY

1 Brigit (Celtic Earth-Mother and goddess of fire, wisdom, poetry, and sacred wells).

2 Juno Februa.

5 Tyche, Fortuna, Wyrd, Ia.

6 Aphrodite (Greek goddess of love).

9 Apollo.

10 Anaitis (Persian goddess of the moon).

12 Artemis, Diana.

14 Vali (Norse archer-god), Juno Februa, Juno Lupa (Roman she-wolf goddess).

15 Faunus, Lupercus.

17 Kali (Hindu destroyer-goddess).

18 Tacita (Roman goddess of silence), Spandarmat (Persian goddess).

19 Minerva, Nammu, Nina.

22 Concordia.

23 Terminus (Roman god of boundaries).

24 Shiva (Hindu god of destruction and renewal).

28 Zamyaz (ancient Persian deity) and the Earth-Goddesses Ceres, Demeter, Gaia, Ge, and Mauri.

MARCH

1 Juno Lucina, Granny March (Bulgarian Witch-Goddess).

2 Ceadda (god of healing springs and sacred wells).

3 Aegir (Teutonic god of the sea), all Triple Goddesses.

4   Rhiannon (Celtic/Welsh Mother Goddess).

5   Isis.

6   Mars, all Roman household gods.

7   Juno.

8   Mother Earth.

11   Herakles (Hercules).

14   Goddess of the Birch Tree, Ua Zit (Egyptian serpent-goddess).

15   Rhea (Greek Earth Goddess).

16   Dionysus, Holika (Indian demon-goddess).

17   Dionysus.

18   Sheela-Na-Gig (Irish fertility goddess).

19   Athena, Minerva, Sitala (Indian goddess).

20   Iduna (Norse goddess), Fortuna, the Morrigan, the Norns, the Three Fates, and the Three Mothers (Lakshmi, Parvati, and Sarasvati).

21   Aries (god of battle).

22   Eostre (Saxon fertility goddess), Ostara (German fertility goddess), the Green Goddess, Lord of the Greenwood.

23   Mars, Saturn.

24   Prytania (Britannia), Heimdall, Cybele.

27   Liber Pater (Roman god of wine), Gauri (Indian goddess of marriage).

28   Kwan Yin, Rudra.

29   Ishtar, all African gods of rain and harvest.

30   Janus, Concordia.

31   Luna (Roman goddess of the moon).

APRIL

1   Loki (Norse trickster-god).

3   Persephone.

4   Cybele (the Great Mother).

5   Fortuna, Kuan Yin.

7   The Blajini (Rumanian spirit-gods of both water and the underworld).

9   A-Ma (Portuguese patroness of fishermen), all Amazon goddesses.

10 Bau (Babylonian goddess and mother of Ea).

11 Anahit (Armenian goddess of love).

12 Ceres (Roman goddess of the fruitful Earth), Chu-Si-Niu, (Taiwanese goddess who presides over the birth of mortals).

13 Libertas (Roman goddess of liberty).

14 Maryamma (Mariamne), all Hindu sea-gods.

15 Tellus Mater (Mother Earth).

16 Apollo.

17 Machendrana (Himalayan rain-god).

18 Rama (Hindu god) and Sita.

20 All bull-gods.

21 Pales (Roman pastoral deity).

22 Gaia (Mother Earth).

23 Jupiter, Venus (Roman goddess of love).

24 Luna Regia (Gnostic lunar-goddess).

27 Tyi Wara (African god of agriculture).

28 Flora (Roman goddess of flowers).

30 Walpurga (Saxon goddess whom the Walpurgisnacht sabbat is named after).

MAY

1 Maia (Roman goddess of springtime).

2 Elena (Helen, goddess of the holy road), Ysahodhara (consort of Buddha).

3 Bona Dea.

4 All Irish fairy-folk.

5 All Mexican and Central American rain-goddesses.

6 Buddha.

7 Apollo.

8 The Horned God (Wiccan).

9 The Lemures.

10 Shiva and his consort Meenakshi, Tin Hau (Chinese goddess of the North Star).

12 Aranya Sashti (Indian god of woodlands).

14 The ancient Norse goddess of the sun, Ing (hearth-god).

15 Maia, Mercury, Vesta (goddess of the hearth).
17 Dea Dia (goddess of the cosmos).
18 Apollo.
20 Thor, Athena.
23 Flora, Venus.
24 Hermes Trismegistus (the patron of alchemists), Artemis (Greek lunar-goddess who also presided over wild beasts and the art of hunting), the Three Celtic Mothers.
25 Apollo.
27 Diana, Proserpina, the Three Fates.
28 Python (Greek serpent-goddess).
29 Ceres, Dea Dia, Mars.
30 Frigg (Norse Queen of Heaven).
31 Buddha.

JUNE

1 Carna (Roman goddess of doors and locks), Tempestas (a powerful ancient goddess who controlled storms).
2 Mother Earth, Ishtar, Apollo.
3 Befana, Bona Dea, Kuan Yin, Rumina, and Surabhi.
5 Domna (Irish goddess of sacred stones), the Rain People, and the Earth Mothers (Native American).
6 Bendi (lunar-goddess of the Balkan Peninsula).
7 Vesta.
8 Mens (Roman goddess of the mind), all Chinese grain-gods.
9 Vesta.
11 Fortuna.
12 Zeus (the most powerful of Greek gods).
13 Athena.
14 Vidar (son of the Norse god Odin), Minerva, Jagannath (a benevolent incarnation of the Indian god Vishnu).
17 Eurydice (Greek tree nymph/underworld-goddess).
18 Anna (Roman goddess).
20 Cerridwen (Celtic goddess of fertility).
21 Hera, Kupala (Russian fertility goddess).

23   The Green Man (ancient Pagan fertility-god).
24   Fortuna.
25   Parvati (Indian goddess).
26   Salavi (Native American spruce tree/rain-god), the Corn
     Mothers and the Kachinas.
27   God of the Summer Sun (Native American, Plains tribe).
28   Hemera (Greek goddess of day).
29   Frey, Freyja, Papa Legba (Voodoo god of crossroads).
30   Aestas (Roman corn-goddess of summer), Ceres, Changing
     Woman (Native American), Chicomecoatl (Aztec), the Corn
     Mothers, Demeter, Gaia, Ge, Hestia, Iatiku, Oraea,
     Pachamama, Spider Woman (Native American), and Tonantzin.

JULY

 1   The Nagas (snake-gods of Nepal), Fuji (Japanese goddess of fire).
 2   All Pagan gods and goddesses who preside over birth and
     fertility.
 3   The Witch of Gaeta, Athena.
 4   Lady Liberty, Pax.
 5   Maat (Egyptian goddess of wisdom and inner truth).
 6   All horned goddesses.
 7   Consus (Roman god of the harvest), Caprotina (goddess of the
     fig tree).
 8   Sunna (Norse goddess of the sun).
 9   Dionysus, Rhea.
10   Holda, Hela, Skadi (European goddesses of the underworld).
11   Kronos (Father Time), Rhea (Mother Earth).
12   Yama (Buddhist god of death and the underworld), Dikai-
     osune (ancient Pagan deity who presided over justice).
13   Osiris (brother and consort of the Egyptian goddess Isis).
14   Horus.
15   Rowana (or Rauni, goddess of the sacred rowan tree), Set
     (Egyptian god of darkness and the magickal arts), Ti-Tsang
     (Chinese god of the underworld).
16   Erzulie Freda (Voodoo goddess of love).

17 Amaterasu (Chinese sun-goddess).
18 Lu Pan (Chinese patron of carpenters), Nepthys (goddess of death), Arstat, Copper Woman (Native American).
19 Isis, Adonis, Aphrodite.
20 All Lithuanian love-goddesses.
23 Neptune (god of the sea) and his consort Salacia, Sulis (goddess of hot springs).
24 All lion-gods.
25 Furrina (ancient Italian goddess of springs).
26 Kachinas (Native American, Hopi tribe).
28 Domhnach Chrom Dubh (Irish sacrificial-god).
29 Thunor, Thor.
30 Gloosca (the Father God, Micmac Indian tribe).
31 Loki and his consort Sigyn, Lugh (Celtic solar deity).

AUGUST

1 Odin, Frigg.
2 Anahita (Persian love-goddess, also a deity associated with the moon).
6 Elihino (Cherokee Earth-Goddess) and her sister Igaehindvo (goddess of the sun), Teinne (or Tan, Celtic personification of holy fire).
7 Adonis, Hathor.
8 Venus.
9 All elemental spirits of Fire.
11 Oddudua (Santerian Mother-Goddess), Robin Goodfellow (through August 14).
12 Isis.
13 Hecate (Greek moon-goddess, Crone, and the protectress of all Witches).
15 Arrianrhod (Celtic Mother-Goddess), Vesta.
17 Diana
19 Venus, Minerva.
21 Hercules.
22 Nu Kwa (Chinese goddess of healing).

23 Nemesis (Greek goddess of fate), Vertumnus (Roman god of the changing seasons), Vulcan (Roman god of volcanic eruptions), and the Nymphs.
25 Ops (Roman goddess of sowing and reaping).
26 Krishna, Ilmatar (Finnish Water-Mother).
27 Consus (Roman god of the grain-store), Devaki (ancient Indian Mother-Goddess).
28 Nephthys (Egyptian goddess of death).
29 Augustus, Hathor (Egyptian goddess of love), Ahes, and Urda of the Three Norns.
30 Tari Pennu (Indian Earth-Goddess).
31 Ananta (Indian Serpent-Goddess).

SEPTEMBER

2 Ariadne, Dionysus.
3 The Maidens of the Four Directions (Hopi tribe).
4 Changing Woman (Native American, Apache tribe).
5 Jupiter (through September 13), Ganesh (Hindu elephant-god of good luck and prosperity).
7 Daena (Maiden-Goddess of the Parsees).
9 Cernunnos (Horned-God).
13 Jupiter, Juno, Minerva, Nephthys.
17 Demeter.
19 Gula (Babylonian goddess of birth), Thoth (Egyptian god of both wisdom and the magickal arts).
20 Quetzalcoatl (Aztec fertility-god).
21 The Egyptian Threefold Goddess (the Mother, the Daughter, and the Dark Mother), Athena.
22 Persephone.
23 Carpo (goddess of autumn), Carman (goddess of poetry).
24 Obatala (Yoruban hermaphrodite deity).
25 Sedna (Eskimo goddess of both the sea and the underworld), Apollo, the Horae (Greek goddess of the four seasons).
26 Theseus (deified Greek hero), Azazel (Hebrew).
27 The Moon Hare (Chinese lunar deity).

28 Demeter (through October 3).
29 Gwynn ap Nudd (Celtic god of both the underworld and the faerie kingdom), Heimdall (Norse god).
30 Medetrina (Roman goddess of medicine and healing).

OCTOBER

1   Fides (Roman goddess who personified faithfulness).
2   All spirit guides.
3   Dionysus, Bacchus (god of wine and mirth-making).
4   Ceres.
5   Old Woman (Lithuanian corn-goddess), Dionysus, Ariadne, the Maenads.
6   Vishnu.
7   Pallas Athena, Victoria (Roman goddess who personified success and triumph).
9   Felicitas (Roman goddess who bestowed good luck upon mortals).
11 Old Lady of the Elder Trees (Germany and Denmark).
12 Fortuna Redux (Roman goddess of journeys and safe returns).
14 Durga (Mother-Goddess).
15 Mars.
16 Lakshmi (goddess of fortune).
17 Tyr (Anglo-Saxon god of the battlefield).
18 Pandrosos (Greek goddess), Cernunnos.
19 The seven Shinto gods of good luck (Japanese).
21 Ursala (Slavic goddess of the moon).
24 Arrianrhod, Carde, Dione, Diti, Gula, Lilith, Maat, Minerva, Sophia.
25 Castor and Pollux (sons of the Greek god Zeus).
28 Baal of the Heavens (Phoenician solar deity), Isis (through November 3).
30 Xipe Totec (Mexican god of death), Tonantzin (Guadualupe goddess of mercy).
31 Cerridwen, Eurydice, Hecate, Hel, Inanna, Kali, the Morrigan, Nephthys, Oya, Samia, Sedna, Tara, Vanadis.

NOVEMBER

1   Pomona, Cailleach (Celtic Crone-Goddess).
2   Woden.
6   Tiamat (Babylonian Dragon-Mother).
7   Hecate, Lono (Hawaiian god).
8   The Manes (Greek spirits of the underworld), Hettsui No Kami (Japanese kitchen-range goddess).
9   Helena, the Four Crowned Martyrs.
10 Nincnevin (Scottish goddess), Reason (French goddess).
11 The Einherjar (spiritual warriors who protect the gods), and the Irish Lunantishees (spirit guardians of the blackthorn tree), Bacchus.
12 Jupiter.
13 Feronia, Juno, Minerva, Jupiter.
14 Moccas (Celtic fig tree-goddess), and the Indian children's goddesses: Befana, Mayauel, Rumina, and Surabhi.
15 Ferona (ancient goddess of fire, fertility and woodlands).
16 Threefold Goddess (Wicca), Lakshmi.
18 Ardvi (Persian goddess, Mother of the Stars).
20 Demeter.
21 Kukulcan (Mayan god), Chango, Damballah, Quetzalcoatl, Tammuz.
22 Ullr (god of wintertime and archery).
23 Konohana-Hime (Japanese granddaughter-goddess of Amaterasu).
24 All Egyptian goddesses of light and birth.
25 Persephone, Proserpina, Kore, Arrianrhod, Catherine (Queen of the Shades).
26 All Tibetan gods of light and fire.
27 Gujeswari (Indian Mother-Goddess), Mother of the Universe (an Indian Triple Goddess whose three aspects are Sarasvati, Lakshmi, and Parvati).
28 Sophia.
29 The sons of the god Saturn.
30 Andros (the divine personification of manhood), Skadi (Scottish goddess).

December

1   Poseidon.
2   All patron goddesses of Japanese craftswomen.
3   Cybele, Bona Dea (the Good Goddess).
4   Minerva, Chango (Yoruban god of lightning bolts).
5   Poseidon, Lucina (Pagan goddess of light who was later Christianized into Saint Lucia).
7   Demeter.
8   Astraea (Greek goddess of justice), Amaterasu, Neith (ancient Egyptian Earth-Goddess of the Delta).
9   Tonantzin.
10   Liberty (goddess of freedom).
11   Bruma (Roman goddess of the winter season), Arrianrhod, the Snow Queen Goddess, and Yuki Onne.
12   Coatlique, Tonantzin, the Black Madonna.
13   Lucina (Sweden).
15   Alcyone (Greek goddess).
16   Sapientia (or Sophia, goddess of wisdom), Athena, Kista, Maat, Minerva, the Shekinah, Spider Woman (Hopi tribe), Hawk Maiden (Hopi tribe).
17   Saturn (through December 24).
18   Diev (Latvian god), Epona (Celtic Mother-Goddess and the patroness of horses).
19   Ops, Sankrant (Hindu goddess).
21   The Horned God.
23   Laurentina (Roman mother of the Lares), Balomain (Kalish demi-god).
25   Invicti Solis (ancient Roman solar deity, the Invincible Sun), Lutzelfrau and Perchta (German Yuletide Witches).
26   Frau Sonne, Igaehindvo, the Star Faery, Sunne, Yemaya.
27   Freya (Norse goddess of fertility, love, and beauty).
29   Andromeda, Ariadne, Artemis.
31   Hogmagog (Scottish god of the sun).

APPENDIX B

INCENSES AND THE SABBATS WITH WHICH THEY ARE ASSOCIATED

The following is a list of twenty-two different incenses, followed by the Sabbat or Sabbats with which they are traditionally associated:

AFRICAN VIOLET: Spring Equinox
ALOES: Lammas
APPLE: Samhain
BASIL: Candlemas
BAYBERRY: Winter Solstice
BENZOIN: Autumn Equinox
CEDAR: Winter Solstice
FRANKINCENSE: Beltane
HELIOTROPE: Samhain
JASMINE: Spring Equinox
LEMON: Summer Solstice
LILAC: Beltane
MINT: Samhain
MYRRH: Candlemas, Summer Solstice, Autumn Equinox
NUTMEG: Samhain
PINE: Summer Solstice, Winter Solstice
ROSE: Spring Equinox, Beltane, Summer Solstice, Lammas
ROSEMARY: Winter Solstice

SAGE: Spring Equinox, Autumn Equinox, Samhain
SANDALWOOD: Lammas
STRAWBERRY: Spring Equinox
WISTERIA: Candlemas, Summer Solstice

BIBLIOGRAPHY

Campanelli, Pauline. *Wheel of the Year: Living the Magical Life.* St. Paul: Llewellyn Publications, 1995.

Dunwich, Gerina. *The Concise Lexicon of the Occult.* New York: Citadel Press, 1990.

————. *The Magick of Candleburning.* New York: Citadel Press, 1989.

————. *The Wicca Book of Days.* New York: Citadel Press, 1995.

Griffon, T. Wynne. *History of the Occult.* New York: Mallard Press, 1991.

Lady Sabrina. *Cauldron of Transformation: A New Vision of Wicca.* St. Paul: Llewellyn Publications, 1996.

Shaw, Eva. *Divining the Future: Prognostication from Astrology to Zoomancy.* New York: Facts on File, 1995.

Simms, Maria Kay. *The Witch's Circle: Rituals and Craft of the Cosmic Muse.* St. Paul: Llewellyn Publications, 1996 (second edition).

Telesco, Patricia. *Spinning Spells, Weaving Wonders: Modern Magic for Everyday Life.* Freedom: Crossing Press, 1996.

INDEX

INDEX

INDEX

INDEX

Unction, 145
Unguent, 145

Valentine spell for Lovers, 90–91
Virgil, 122
Visualization, 119, 121, 145

Wand, 145
Waning Moon, 5–6, 85, 121
Warlock, 145
Watchtowers, 145
Waxing Moon, 4–5, 85, 121
Weatherworking, 145
Wheel of the Year, 23–44
White, 52, 55
Wiccan/Pagan organizations, 151
Wiccan/Pagan publications, 152
Wiccan Rede, 147
Widdershins, 147
Winter Solstice, 24, 29–30, 69,
    114–15
Witch bottle, 147
Witch hole, 147
Witchcraft (defined), 147–48
Wortcunning, 148

Yellow, 53–53, 57
Yule log, 91

Zodiac, 7, 44

Free Catalog
of New Age & Occult Books From Carol Publishing Group

For over 30 years, the Citadel Library of the Mystic Arts has been hailed as America's definitive line of works on Wicca and White Magic, Occult Sciences and Personalities, Demonology, Spiritism, Mysticism, Natural Health, Psychic Sciences, Witchcraft, Metaphysics, and Esoterica.

Selected titles include: The Alexander Technique • Amulets and Talismans • Apparitions and Survival of Death • Astral Projection • At the Heart of Darkness • The Bedside Book of Death • Beyond the Light • The Book of Ceremonial Magic • The Book of Spells, Hexes, and Curses • The Book of the Dead • Buddha and the Gospel of Buddhism • Candlelight Spells • The Candle Magick Workbook • The Case for Reincarnation • Classic Vampire Stories • The Complete Guide to Alternative Cancer Therapies • The Concise Lexicon of the Occult • Cosmic Consciousness • Daily Meditations for Dieters • Deceptions and Myths of the Bible • The Dictionary of Astrology • Dracula Book of Great Horror Stories • Egyptian Magic • Egyptian Religion • An Encyclopedia of Occultism • Encyclopedia of Signs, Omens and Superstitions • Everyday Wicca • The Fairy-Faith in Celtic Countries • From Elsewhere • Future Memory • The Grim Reaper's Book of Days • Gypsy Sorcery and Fortune Telling • A History of Secret Societies • The History of Witchcraft • The Hollow Earth • The Holy Kabbalah • How to Improve Your Psychic Power • How to Interpret Your Dreams From A - Z • How To Make Amulets, Charms and Talismans • Hypnosis • Inner Peace in a 9-5 World • The Kabbalah • Know Your Body Clock • The Lost Language of Symbolism, Vols. 1 & 2 • The Magick of Candle Burning • The Magus • Meaning in Dreams and Dreaming • The Modern Witch's Book of Home Remedies • The Modern Witch's Dreambook • The Modern Witch's Spellbook, 1 & 2 • Moon Madness • Not of This World • Numerology • Our Earth, Our Cure • Out-of-the-Body Experiences • The Pictorial Key to the Tarot • The Practice of Witchcraft Today • Principles of Light and Color • Rituals of Renewal • The Roots of Healing • Satanism • Satanism and Witchcraft • The Secrets of Ancient Witchcraft • Shouting at the Wolf • Strange World • Study and Practice of Astral Projection • The Symbolism of Color • The Talisman Magick Workbook • Tarot Cards • Teachings of Tibetan Yoga • A Treasury of Witchcraft • The Vampire • The Werewolf of Paris • What Happens When You Die • Where the Ghosts Are • The Wicca Book of Days • Wicca Candle Magick • Wicca Craft • The Wicca Garden • Wicca Love Spells • Wicca Sourcebook • Wicca Spellbook • Wiccan Prophecy • Window To the Past • Witchcraft • Witchcraft, Sorcery, and Superstition • You Are All Sanpaku • Zen Macrobiotic Cooking

Ask for these New Age and Occult books at your bookstore. To order direct or to request a brochure, call 1-800-447-BOOK or send your name and address to Carol Publishing Group, 120 Enterprise Avenue, Dept 1869, Secaucus, NJ 07094.

Prices subject to change; books subject to availability